THE PRESSURE PRINCIPLE

Handle Stress, Harness Energy, and Perform When It Counts

DR DAVE ALRED MBE

PENGUIN LIFE

AN IMPRINT OF

PENGUIN BOOKS

PENGUIN LIFE

UK | USA | Canada | Ireland | Australia
India | New Zealand | South Africa

Penguin Life is part of the Penguin Random House group of companies
whose addresses can be found at global.penguinrandomhouse.com.

First published 2016
001

Copyright © Dave Alred, 2016

The moral right of the author has been asserted

Set in 10/13.5 pt ITC Stone Serif Std
Typeset by Jouve (UK), Milton Keynes
Printed in Great Britain by Clays Ltd, St Ives plc

A CIP catalogue record for this book is available from the British Library

ISBN: 978–0–241–24084–7

This book is dedicated to all those
who think they can't

CONTENTS

INTRODUCTION

Under Pressure

At the end of a long and stressful week at work, you've finally completed your report. You gather up the crumpled pages of notes that have been your crutch for the last few days and screw them into a ball before leaning back in your chair and tossing them towards the waste bin on the other side of your office.

Bullseye! You congratulate yourself on a perfectly judged throw. *Everyone's a champion when no one else is looking.*

Jack, a colleague, walks in, smiling mischievously. 'A pound says you can't make that throw again,' he says.

'You're on.' The stakes are low, your confidence is high and the shot is makeable. You take aim . . .

'Woah, not so fast, hot shot,' interrupts Jack. 'Let's make this a bit more interesting.'

Jack heads down the corridor to summon everyone on your floor, offering them bets on the throw, telling them it's easy money – that you'll never make the shot from twenty feet. Soon, your office has more people in than ever before and the jar containing the stake money is half full. It doesn't stop there.

In his new role as bookmaker, Jack spreads the word – news travels fast in this company – and before long it's out of control: your office is rammed, people are crowding the corridors and pressing up against the windows and bets are being laid thick and fast.

'I've got a fiver on this,' pipes up someone.

'Put me down for ten,' says another.

Of course, you can't back down, so you take every bet thrown your way. Even the CEO gets in on the act, wagering a cool fifty quid that you won't make it. The chatter is incessant, the tension palpable and the pot is swelling at just over a thousand pounds as Jack finally closes the book and, like an admonishing umpire at Wimbledon, calls for, 'Quiet, please.'

A hush descends. All eyes turn to you. One shot for glory.

You take the paper ball – it feels alien and unfamiliar between your palms – and roll it tighter, thinking about how best to make the throw, about what happens if you don't. *A thousand pounds!* Your palms feel clammy, your chest is tight, your heart pounding.

The eyes of your colleagues bore into you. This is it: your putt for victory in the Ryder Cup, the last-minute penalty to win a World Cup final. Your chance to make office history.

With dry mouth and knotted stomach, you take back your arm. *How did I do it before?* You try to visualize it going in the bin as you bring your arm forward and release the paper ball. It leaves your hand and the room draws breath as it arcs through the air . . .

Pressure Defined

We all have our own definition of pressure. For some it's the pressure to present to a new client at work. For others it's the stresses involved in running their own business. Many of us face the pressure to juggle long hours at work with being a good parent at home and plenty know all too well the pressure to make ends meet. It's not just this objectively serious kind of pressure we can relate to. We can feel pressure when we're meeting people for the first time, be they new colleagues at work or a partner's social group, or even in moments when we might feel silly for getting worked up, such as waiting at the start of our own birthday party for people to arrive. We can put ourselves under immense pressure to achieve when we tackle things like running a marathon or performing in an event that matters to us – whether in a five-a-side football tournament, a local play or even throwing a ball of paper into a bin. Pressure can create a very personal kind of pain.

Yet although it means different things to different people, and can affect us in a variety of ways, we all recognize its effects in ourselves and others. People under pressure nearly always betray symptoms. Some are better than others at managing them or hiding them, but we recognize their imprint. And outside our own social sphere, when we watch sport and films and television programmes, we can see it there. We're familiar with the toll it takes – be it on a player trying to pot an easy-looking black to win the World Snooker Championship or an onscreen hero trying to defuse a bomb – because we feel pressure in our own lives, albeit usually on a more modest stage and in less perilous circumstances. Sport and drama magnify the tensions we know all too well from first-hand experience.

Pressure means something different to everyone, so how might we begin to define it clearly as something we can all understand? You might think a dictionary would be a good place to start, but it's easy to become lost in the many definitions that don't quite tap into the core of what it is that we all *feel* when facing pressure. And that is where our attentions should be directed. It is the *effects* of pressure that concern us, that inhibit us. How is it that some of us can deliver a great performance when it matters most while others visibly wilt under the strain?

Anxiety, elevated heart rate, sweating, feeling 'tight' in the shoulders or neck, headaches, butterflies and nausea are just some of the physical symptoms we can experience as a result of pressure. The mental effects can be just as pronounced: our confidence, concentration, memory, emotional control, decision-making, sense of perspective, ability to remain present and in the moment can all be compromised when we're under pressure, preventing us from doing something we might manage easily in a more relaxed environment.

Top-level sportsmen experience these effects just like the rest of us, and professional sport is littered with expressions such as 'performance anxiety' and 'choking'. Of course, they have learned, using some of the methods I will describe in this book, how to manage these effects better than many – performing in front of thousands of people regularly will do that to a person. But anyone who has watched a penalty shootout will know that no one is immune to pressure – not even the very best.

Pressure gets the better of everyone at some point. Which of us can honestly say we haven't underperformed in an exam, interview, social engagement or at work because of nerves? Pressure on us when we do these things, whether for professional, social or simply survival reasons, inhibits and challenges our ability to make decisions. So for the purposes of this book, let's take a clear, simple definition of pressure, in the knowledge that it isn't pressure itself that's the problem – it's the impact it has on us:

PRESSURE *The interference with the ability to concentrate on a process, consciously or subconsciously, causing deterioration in technique and decreasing the level of performance.*

So in your efforts to throw the ball into the bin in your office, the pressure arises from (a) the thought of losing a lot of money (you had over £1,000 resting on the outcome); (b) having to perform in front of a large audience, many of whom you don't know; and (c) having to deliver in front of your CEO – effectively, the pressure of being able to deliver under pressure.

The fact that you succeeded when you thought no one was looking is of little help when faced with such a crowd of people. You've had no real practice in these conditions, no conscious process or learned technique that will give you the best chance of success. You have to get it right first time.

Pressure – the Philosophy

If I had to give a high-concept appraisal of my coaching philosophy, it would be: 'To rekindle youthful learning and create a "no limits" mindset.'

No matter who you are – the world's number-one golfer, a nurse in an overburdened A&E department, rugby's best goal kicker or one employee among thousands in a big company – you can always improve. At the margins of your performance, you can still get better – and you can learn to enjoy and embrace the challenge of improving and celebrate your progress.

Elite-level sport distils perfectly and most purely the ideas and preconceptions we hold about pressure. Where else would a player have to take a penalty in a full stadium, with millions watching on television, to win a tournament that comes around only every four years and which might be the player and team's sole chance ever to win it?

In sport the margins are so fine and yet the outcomes are so black and white: winners and losers. Only in sport do we collectively and publicly witness the effects of pressure at its most extreme. They can be the best in the world but still miss a simple kick from twelve yards, a three-foot putt or an easy pot, or double fault at a crucial juncture. For all the extreme pressure that paramedics, soldiers, firemen, police officers and the like are under – where decisions can literally be a matter of life and death, unlike Bill Shankly's famous quote about football – their often heroic, dangerous and breathtaking activities aren't in a public arena. No audience will judge how well they respond to pressure. Similarly, those in less dangerous but very stressful professions such as investment bankers, lawyers and stockbrokers don't regularly perform their duties under the gaze of TV cameras – even if some of us might appreciate knowing exactly what is going on behind their doors.

It is in sport, then, where the application and consequences of pressure are crystal clear, that the phenomenon can most easily be studied and understood. Sport is our public portal into the physical and psychological torment pressure can wreak – and into our heroes who are best able to manage and harness its effects for both personal glory and the glory of their teams.

In a career in sport of over twenty years I've been fortunate enough to meet and learn from many great coaches and players. I have worked with, among others, rugby internationals Jonny Wilkinson and Johnny Sexton, star golfers Luke Donald and Padraig Harrington, and several elite teams, including the England rugby squad, the British and Irish Lions, the British Judo Association and, from Australian Rules football, West Coast Eagles. I've also worked with players who aren't household names but are just as committed to embracing the challenge to improve at their own level, in their own way and at their own margins. Helping them develop has been equally satisfying. And it is in sport – specifically, golf – where I have worked on my own improvement, rediscovering my empathy with the angst and pressures involved in learning and mastering any new skill.

Sport, however, is just the jumping-off point. Previously I was a secondary school teacher, working for several years in three large inner-city comprehensive schools in Bristol. On reflection, I am convinced that this teaching experience created the strongest possible foundation to develop my coaching skills. I am hugely grateful to those colleagues who, in this often undervalued profession, supported and encouraged my early development.

I have felt the pressures that a life outside sport can produce. I have learned from both sides, with my work in sport informing my life outside it and vice versa. My search for improvement motivated me to complete a PhD at Loughborough University while also working full-time, which was a great experience but left me with more questions than answers. I'm now asking much better questions.

The Pressure Principle

The Pressure Principle has evolved over the many years I have been teaching, researching and coaching. It is a result of the methodology I have learned, adapted and created in my career in sports such as golf, rugby, cricket, football, judo, polo, Aussie Rules and many more, and of the wealth of experience life has a tendency to throw our way. I've seen first-hand the consequences that extremes of pressure can produce and I've worked hard with people from all walks of life to help them cope.

The Pressure Principle is no quick-fix, sticking-plaster solution; it is a multifaceted philosophy, but its lessons are simple to apply. You'll see benefits in the short term, certainly, and, if you commit to it fully, the long-term gains can be huge. You *will* see improvements. You *will* be better able to deal with pressure and perform at your best.

The Pressure Principle comprises eight intermingled strands, each of which is the subject of a separate chapter:

- **Anxiety** – *the source of many of our issues when confronted with pressure, the physical symptoms of which can be mastered to perform effectively.*
- **Language** – *the lifeblood of all the strands – its power and influence should never be underestimated.*
- **Managing Learning** – *how we can learn more effectively and improve our skills under pressure.*
- **Implicit–Explicit Balance** – *how the balance of information in our minds is kept in equilibrium.*
- **Behaviour** – *the power of effective practice.*
- **Environment** – *how we can manage our expectations and surroundings when the pressure's on.*
- **Sensory Shutdown** – *what happens to our minds and bodies when extreme pressure hits us, and how we can delay its impact.*

- **Thinking Correctly Under Pressure** – *the final component to complete the Pressure Principle.*

These eight strands are all interrelated, so there isn't a neat cut-off between each of them; instead, they feed into one another: seven intertwining strands woven around the common thread of language.

This book examines not only the importance of practice per se, but also how different types of practice can prepare us for the pressured environment. It explains both how a skill is learned in the first place and the most effective ways to execute it when the tension mounts. Techniques are offered to build confidence and develop a productive mindset to tackle the mental interference that might inhibit us at crucial moments in our lives. The power of the body, as well as the mind, to help us cope with stress will be explained, too. Going beyond sport, we will look at what we can learn from the Royal Marines, dolphin trainers, fighter pilots, skateboarders, car salesmen and the world of advertising.

My hope is that anyone wanting to improve their performance in a pressured environment will be helped by this book. My message is that you are capable of achieving so much more, whoever you are. I don't have all the answers – I too subscribe to the no-limits mindset and am always learning and keen to improve – but I am about to share the results of my experience as a teacher, a learner and a coach to some of the best in the world in the most pressured environments imaginable.

1. ANXIETY

1.

Synchronizing the Butterflies

Towards the end of 2011, English golfer Luke Donald was on the verge of making history. If he were to finish high enough in the Dubai World Championship, he would become the first player in the history of the game to top the money lists on both sides of the Atlantic – on the US PGA and European tours. His main rival in Dubai was the US Open champion Rory McIlroy, who could also still top the money list.

Luke was clearly feeling the pressure. His demeanour reminded me of Jonny Wilkinson's before playing rugby for England: very quiet and focused. I travelled with Luke to the course daily and, before his final and decisive round, I wrote him a motivational note – to give clear, uncomplicated direction. It finished with:

Tall in execution and singularly ruthless in mind – feeling excited/ nervous, maybe uncomfortable – it's great – it's your fuel for a great performance – a BIG performance.

That was exactly what he produced. Luke went round six under par and, as Rory McIlroy fell away, Luke finished top of the European money list – the Race to Dubai – securing his place in history and consolidating his number-one world ranking, which he had wrested from countryman Lee Westwood at the PGA Championships at Wentworth earlier in the year.

Even though his energy levels for the last two days of the tournament weren't as high as they had been, Luke had still been fully committed in the gym and produced some outstanding numbers in practice. And then he had delivered where it mattered – an incredible achievement.

It wasn't until the following year, when he was being interviewed at the same event in Dubai, that he revealed he hadn't enjoyed the 2011 experience at all. He said that there had been too much pressure.

Feeling Anxious

Whether it's the familiar feelings of Sunday night dread before a tough week at work or butterflies in your stomach before an exam, we all experience feelings of anxiety. While we often have good reason to be anxious when we are, say, expecting test results from a doctor or we're waiting outside an operating theatre with a loved one inside, anxiety more often than not in our everyday lives involves the *perception* of a threat, rather than an actual physical threat to ourselves.

In his book *Sport and Exercise Psychology: The Key Concepts*, Ellis Cashmore details several forms of anxiety, which are all related to:

> *a general emotional and cognitive reaction to a particular stimulus or environment in which apprehension and trepidation are present.*

It's this *reaction*, based on our individual perceptions, that explains why one person could see a particular situation as an eagerly awaited test of their mettle – a challenge to rise up and meet – while another could feel threatened and subsequently unable to perform to the best of their ability to deal with it. What we perceive as being threatening differs from person to person, and it is our perceptions that are generating the anxiety rather than the situation itself.

The two main forms of anxiety are *trait* anxiety and *state* anxiety. Trait anxiety, as the name suggests, describes someone's general level of anxiety, rather than a response to a temporary situation. Someone who experiences high levels of trait anxiety in the company of others would find a range of objectively non-threatening circumstances stressful, such as going to work every day or attending a birthday party.

State anxiety, however, is a temporary condition which describes the stresses involved when someone perceives specific situations as threatening. The anxiety usually disappears after the challenge has been faced, but it can cause a lot of problems before and during the event, which can severely compromise performance. Perhaps you usually enjoy work, but the fact that you have a big presentation in front of the board today could be making you extremely anxious indeed.

State anxiety is the form of anxiety I tackle in my work, as it is usually experienced around specific events and situations that we need to address. (Many people in the sporting world prefer the term 'performance anxiety'.) An otherwise confident person might go to pieces on the golf course, where state anxiety strikes. Or they could be a pretty good golfer until their ball ends up in a bunker – a specific situation within the game. State anxiety usually occurs when we attempt a challenge outside our comfort zone, such as playing in a cup final or giving your first presentation to your new classmates at university.

Performance Anxiety

It is generally accepted that anxiety – the perception of a threat – produces tension in the body and can create all manner of emotional distractions that can put us off the task at hand. These task-irrelevant thoughts interfere with our thinking and prevent us from being able to perform efficiently a process we would otherwise be able to do easily. For an elite sportsman, this might mean an inability to execute a well-practised, basic motor skill and make sound decisions.

If we return to our example of throwing a ball of paper at a bin, how much would the burgeoning audience and the financial pressure have brought about an unhelpful emotional state in you? Would you have thrived under it, or would your arm have grown heavy, your mind overwhelmed by unhelpful thoughts? Would you have experienced state anxiety?

This kind of anxiety can manifest itself in many ways, including extreme self-consciousness and overthinking how you'd throw the paper ball, as well as the usual physical symptoms: the pounding heart, dry mouth and sweating. But at its core, the causes are quite simple: it's a fear of failure.

The 'f' word has become an all too powerful part of our language. It allows us to paint things in black and white and, despite our best efforts, it is easy to view anything in which we don't 100 per cent succeed as 'failure'. Yes, failure can lead to all sorts of problems: failure in the case of your paper-ball throw would have real financial repercussions for you, while in an exam or a test, failure is usually easily defined. But 'failure' can mean all sorts of things in other situations and include many shades of grey. It could mean meeting a new partner's social group for the first time when you're nervous about it and feeling afterwards that you haven't given a good account of yourself. It could mean volunteering to give a talk at your local school, only to have a class full of bored children horsing around and playing on their phones instead of listening to you.

Not all of these 'failures' have huge, negative consequences. Some of them are learning experiences and, most interestingly, it is quite often the case that 'failure' in our own minds isn't even detectable by others, who might think everything went fine. Your partner might say, 'You were great – who wouldn't be a bit nervous and uncomfortable with a room full of strangers basically interrogating them?' An experienced teacher might simply smile and say, 'Welcome to my world!'

Again, this is all pointing to our *perception* of a situation. We're negatively reinforcing (our own) subjective opinions rather than objective truths. Unfortunately, once we perceive that we've failed, we're more likely to be anxious about doing it again, and for some people that then means they start trying to avoid the situation – avoiding the possibility of failure.

When we see this on the sports field, we talk about teams and players looking to evade defeat rather than striving for victory. And once these kinds of thoughts come into play, it exerts a different kind of pressure, more difficult to manage.

Don't Miss!

I regularly work with Kevin Shine, the England and Wales Cricket Board's lead fast-bowling coach. We were putting the England performance squad bowlers through a test in which they had to hit a target that was marked as a slot on the floor six yards from the stumps. The slot was two yards long and twelve inches wide. For each hit the bowler scored a point. By the end of the session, all eight of the bowlers were hitting the targets and there was a fair bit of competitive edge between them.

We then changed the contest so that, instead of being rewarded for hitting their target, the bowlers were penalized for *not* landing their ball in the target area, the two-yard by twelve-inch slot. This proved to be a much tougher test, with the bowlers having to adjust from a proactive task, to make a conscious act to *avoid* an outcome. The key for the bowler was to replace the conditions we had created and convert the task in their minds to hitting the target, rather than not missing.

The new contest was simple: miss the two-yard target and you were out. We had two sudden-death rounds, with a victorious bowler left at the end of each. Whereas before there had been a good sense of camaraderie and competition, now the atmosphere shifted and the banter became subdued. The players afterwards spoke of how they had felt much more pressure. The pressure caused the bowler to experience an increase in tension, which made the swing arc tighter and smaller. Of the fourteen balls that missed the target, thirteen were bowled short.

The difference between moving *towards* something – wanting to achieve it – and moving *away* from something – not wanting to fail – can have a significant impact on the way we think. When it is applied to an event or even a single action, such as a specific ball being bowled, then trying not to miss pollutes the brain with the idea of the ball missing its target. Trying *not* to muck up your exams, your presentation, the interview you're about to go on – it's all planting the idea of failure in your mind. It is far more effective to visualize yourself successfully completing your exams, presentation or interview.

Successful people are more able in the heat of competition to visualize what they want and have the confidence in their technique to focus on what to do, rather than allowing thoughts of what to avoid distract them.

Any Road Will Take You There

A team languishing near the bottom of the Premier League – take Sunderland from 2013–14 or 2014–15 – that has spent almost the entire season down there, suddenly starts putting an immense winning streak together, somehow beating teams near the top of the table in quick succession to avoid relegation. And then what happens when they are safe? Results drop off, performances fall away – and it's hard to escape the feeling that those very teams will be back in the mire again the following season.

At the beginning of February 2016, Sunderland – who won back-to-back games for the first time all season in their last six games of 2014–15, losing just once, when safety was all but secured – were back near the bottom of the table.

So how can such teams briefly demonstrate the kind of form that would see them safely near the top of the table if they maintained it throughout a season?

Those who are motivated by avoidance – who wish to move away from trouble, stress, discomfort or pain – tend only to perform when these threats are near at hand. The further away from the source of discomfort they move – in this case relegation – the less impact it has upon them. They played quite consistently throughout the season and then, when the threat was at its most acute, their motivation increased dramatically; they played out of their skins to save themselves from the ignominy and (relative) poverty of Championship status. Once the threat was gone their motivation went back to its pre-threat levels.

Of course, that's not to say that this kind of performance isn't worthy of merit. Those teams that successfully avoid relegation from such a position are able to perform better than those who are actually relegated when this kind of pressure is on. It is no coincidence that Sunderland had pulled off an even more remarkable escape in the 2013–14 season, leaping from bottom of the table with only six games remaining to win four and draw one of their next five, beating the likes of Chelsea and Manchester United on their own grounds in the process. And it's not just teams at the bottom of the table: if you look at a club like Arsenal's ability to perform when their Champions League qualification is under threat, you can see a similar avoidance motivation (i.e. they're motivated *not* to finish outside of the top four) which is shown in their improved performance when the pressure is on and the fact that they haven't finished outside the Champions League places since the 1996–97 season, when they finished third and only the top two qualified. They are used to finishing there, and they have the experience to draw upon to help them.

Those with a primary motivation to avoid distress and unfavourable outcomes invariably suffer from increased anxiety and stress levels, either individually or as a team. They don't become proactive until the pressure is at its absolute peak. Sound familiar? Many of us are similarly motivated in our day-to-day lives: did you always leave that essay at school until the night before? Do you find yourself preparing for an interview on the way there? Are you up until the small hours filling in your tax return as the deadline is hours away?

It would be much better, in terms of both our health and our performance, to react earlier to these situations, when we would have more practical options available to us. But some people genuinely can't seem to do this – they need the motivating pressure to force them into it, despite the fact that doing so cuts down their options.

This method of dealing with pressure has its limitations. Those who are generally motivated by avoidance usually spend so much time and energy on moving away from the situation that they don't have the resources to plan and work through methods to improve themselves in the long term. I have known of Premier League footballers manipulating situations so that they are able to dodge a specific challenge – choosing the easy pass instead of exposing themselves to potential derision or failure – at a crucial point in the match.

In the workplace, say you struggled with public speaking. If you are motivated by avoidance, you might find yourself doing everything in your power to move away from situations where you'd be required to do it, perhaps avoiding volunteering for potentially career-furthering projects or not applying for a job you might covet, or even delegating public-speaking responsibilities to a junior, which might save you from the short-term threat you perceive but does little to enhance your standing in the eyes of your peers. The energy and effort and the attendant anxiety and stress involved may help you in your short-term goal (avoiding public speaking), but are they making the problem go away? Surely it would be far better to use all that effort to make improvements to your public-speaking skills, to face your problems and take on even a little of the responsibility you've spent so long avoiding.

Avoidance-motivated people spend so much time concentrating on what they *don't* want, rather than what they do, that they have nothing to aim for except staying out of the way of the same things they have always avoided. This will be discussed further in a later chapter, but in the meantime it is safe to assume that the likes of Sunderland will be spending the season with one simple motivation: *not* to get relegated. And, if you're that way inclined, I don't doubt for a second that you'll be up late again doing next year's tax return so that you do *not* miss the deadline.

High Octane Fuel for the Body

It was June 1997 in South Africa, with the British Lions about to play the crucial second Test against their hosts. The changing room was alive with the sounds of metal studs clattering on the concrete floor, of colourful language and shouts of, 'Come on!' from pumped-up players preparing to go into battle . . . and of the unmistakeable sound of retching from the toilets.

Welsh full-back Neil Jenkins would often vomit before games. His state anxiety would see him worked up to the point of having to be sick before the match; however, once on the pitch he was an ice-cold operator, exhibiting no sign of what had been going on before. This Test was no different.

We had worked very hard on Neil's kicking for touch in the week leading up to the match, as we expected a lot of penalties to be awarded. Neil was perfect in his goal kicking in the match and was able to give us the territorial advantage to go for goal more often than the South Africans could kick at ours. Although they scored three tries, Neil put away five penalties to lead the Lions to an 18–15 victory – and with it the series.

The effects of pressure are often not pleasant. As Luke Donald said at the start of the chapter, sometimes they can be so severe that they completely take away the enjoyment of even a successful event. However, in my experience most sportsmen and women wouldn't trade these pre-match emotional responses – the blood racing through the veins, the bouncing off the walls, even the vomiting – for anything.

There is a negativity associated with anxiety and nervousness, and we seem to have the idea that such feelings should be avoided and that they invoke shame. You wouldn't want your colleagues at work or your opponent on the sports field to know about your nerves, to be aware of your 'weakness'. But I believe this is a completely misguided approach. There is another, perhaps more surprising way to approach state anxiety, and that is to *embrace* these feelings.

Adrenaline can be your best friend if you understand how to harness it and learn to accept that it is part of a great performance to come. I have worked with innumerable athletes who maintain that, without anxiety, they wouldn't be able to perform to their potential. So, despite their not being very pleasant, the impact of these feelings before a big event – and it could be an Olympic final, an office football competition or your first day of work after leaving school – can, with effective management, become not only helpful but vital for you to perform much nearer to the best of your ability.

How is it possible to be courageous if you're not at first afraid? It is perfectly natural to experience fear; we have all felt it at some point in our lives and professional athletes are no different, despite what they might claim. But it is not perfectly natural to allow fear to have mastery over us. What often separates the best from the rest is *courage*. Not the audacious acts of bravery more suitable for the silver screen, but rather the smaller, everyday kind that demonstrate the ability to control our fear. And I'm not just talking about sportspeople. No entertainer at any level will ever do well if they can't control their stage fright. No nurse or doctor will last long if they cannot manage their anxiety about making quick, life-or-death decisions. No one working in a pub or restaurant can get through a busy Friday night if they cannot tame their anxiety when faced with groups of unpredictable people.

It is not the amount of fear that is important, then, but the amount of courage we possess to address this fear and utilize it. It is vital to see anxiety as a positive aspect of performance. As Olympic basketball coach Jack Donohue so eloquently expressed it: 'It's not a case of getting rid of the butterflies, it's a question of getting them to fly in formation.'

When I was coaching rugby with England, the goal kickers would practise every day in the week leading up to a match. The kicking practice at the beginning of the week concentrated entirely on accuracy, quality of strike and technique rather than distance. Towards the end of the week, when anxiety levels were increasing in anticipation of the looming match, the kickers would start naturally achieving longer distances, in large part due to the increase in adrenaline. The players called this anxiety 'juice'. They used it as a fuel. We hadn't concentrated on distance earlier in the week as it could have resulted in the players over-exerting to kick the ball too hard, which would interfere with their technique, so a particularly long kick then would be admired because it was 'without juice'. These players – the best in the country – understood implicitly the need for anxiety to fuel their performance.

While state anxiety can be harnessed to enhance performance in the heat of battle, it's not to say the effects prior to the event won't be unpleasant. Neil Jenkins might have been sick before taking the field, but once on it he was a fantastic performer, using his anxiety to improve his play in big games. Someone else who knows a thing or two about performing under pressure, eighteen-time major winner Jack Nicklaus, said:

I don't know how you can play well if you are not nervous. Nowadays I don't get nervous unless I'm in a major and in a position

*to win. If I could only learn to concentrate when I am not nerv-
ous, so I could get into a position to win, I would be fine.*

To a skilled performer, anxiety can be essential. The physical
symptoms, such as the increased heart rate, sweating and muscle
tension as a result of adrenaline, are the 'juice' to produce that
extra bit of distance, slightly faster speed, extra reach, harder
punch – that ability for someone to reach into themselves for a
little more. Without this, complacency can set in. I remember one
occasion with the England rugby team, after the final meeting
and getting on the team coach to head to the ground, discussing
with the rest of the staff whether the players were up for it. Were
they experiencing the anxiety to fuel a big performance?

The release of adrenaline readies the body for fight or flight,
and it is the skilled performer on any stage who has the ability to channel this mode through the execution of a precise,
well-rehearsed series of skills, while the less-practised will not
be able to focus so accurately to utilize this surge of adrenaline. As Donohue said: 'If your focus is in the right place – for
example, on reminding yourself of your best task focus and then
on riveting yourself to that task – the butterflies will fly in
formation.'

But how exactly do we get them to do that?

C to J – Easy as 1, 2, 3?

Picture a city at rush hour: the sun is beating down; cars are grid-
locked, bumper to bumper; horns are blaring – no one is going
anywhere fast. Now look at the drivers: they're over their wheels,
with hunched, tense shoulders, their chins forward and a look of
exasperation on their faces. No wonder tempers are short!

When we're under pressure, we often aren't immediately conscious of the effect it has on our minds – and even more often,
such as in situations like a stressful rush-hour traffic jam, we

aren't aware of the impact it's having on our bodies. The physical effect of long-term stress is well documented, with the likes of hypertension and heart disease the potential consequences, and most of us would like to *think* we'd recognize the immediate impact of short-term anxiety on our bodies. If I asked you to show me what a stressed person looks like, you'd probably adopt a pose like the drivers in the traffic jam: tensed shoulders, hunched over, head down. You'd take on these characteristics and it would feel like a pronounced shift in your body. But if, on another occasion, you were genuinely stressed and I put a mirror in front of you, the chances are you'd be shocked by how much your appearance resembles your impression of a stressed person without your even being aware of it.

When we're under pressure, our heart rate rises and our attention narrows to become consumed by the source of our stress. As a consequence, our awareness of our environment, and especially our *self*-awareness, plummets, so that we can be hunched over, head down, shoulders clenched, displaying all the symptoms of the physical impact of anxiety without even realizing it. So, this is the anxiety in our mind having a subconscious impact on our bodies, affecting our body language. But what we are usually not so blissfully unaware of is just how much the body then, in turn, informs the mind. There is a reciprocal relationship going on, with a stressed mind resulting in a stressed body, the stressed body then making for an even more stressed mind, and so on. The worst of it is, we usually have no idea this is happening, so lost are we in our problems.

This is where the C to J concept comes in. It is a tool I have developed, initially in rugby goal kicking and now use to help manage the physical impact of anxiety in the people I work with. I have used it with everyone from golfers to judo players, from Premier League footballers to polo players and from students to salesmen. At its heart, it is about giving someone the power to use their body language to 'talk' to their mind, raising the awareness and producing a set of characteristics in the body to better reflect a more positive state of mind, all of which should help mobilize your butterflies.

The C to J concept's name comes from its origins as a kicking tool. If you look at Figure 1, drawn from above, you'll see the difference between the C-shape and the J-shape. On the left is plotted the path the foot of a C-shape kicker would take when kicking the ball, in which only a small part of the swing moves through and in the intended direction of the ball. On the right, however, the J-shape plots a kick where the path of the swing goes from curved to straight, spending more time in the intended direction of the ball. The fundamental principle of kicking in all sports is applying power through the ball in the direction in which you want it to travel, for which the J-shape is clearly more effective.

One of the most notable J-shape models is footballer Cristiano Ronaldo, who has a powerful, upright posture and kicking technique. Former England captains Steven Gerrard and David

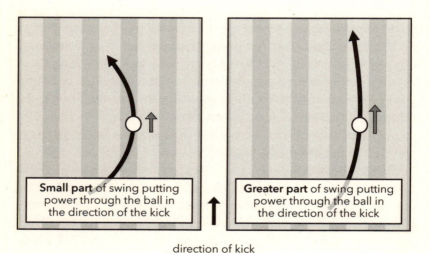

direction of kick

Figure 1 *The C to J principle*

Beckham, on the other hand, are more towards being C-shape kickers.

While all these players have been very successful, it is the J-shape that is more effective for pressure situations. When anxiety starts to have an impact on a player, their muscles naturally begin to tighten. Unchecked, the player is likely to lean towards the C-shape, which produces a more inconsistent strike because the foot's path is going towards the target for only a very small part of its swing. Top players such as those I've mentioned are usually able to deal with the effects of anxiety very well; however, J-shape kickers are more likely to be able to maintain their technique even under extreme conditions. With muscles tightening and movements shortening, it doesn't affect the path: a line is still a line, even if it's shorter, whereas when a circle gets tighter, it changes the path.

Clearly, there are many highly accomplished and successful C-shape kickers in the upper echelons of the games of football and rugby, but I believe they could still improve their consistency. Someone with a 'no-limits' mindset would always believe in their capacity to improve.

Through using the C to J concept in kicking initially and then expanding it into other sports – such as golf, particularly in regards to the swing – and then into areas like business, I have developed a comparison of physical characteristics that are influenced when we experience anxiety (see Table 1).

I use this table primarily as a checklist to see if and how pressure is affecting someone's physical demeanour. Of course, not all of these characteristics are relevant to every activity, just as not all of them are relevant to each individual – people exhibit the physical effects of pressure in many different ways. It isn't a case of the C-shape being inherently bad and the J-shape being good. Very few will have a profile entirely in the C or J column. The point is to use it more as a loose guideline to make people aware of their reactions to the pressured environment, and thus

Table 1 The C to J table

C-shape ←		→ J-shape
Hunched, curled	Posture	Upright, angular
Small	Body	Big
Quick, snatched	Speed	Controlled, in command
Appears rushed	Time	Time to see, decide and execute
Rotates	Pillar	Shifts to target
Straighten	Legs	Knees flexed
Adduction	Principal action	Flexion
Flit	Awareness	Grounded
Anxiety	Emotion	Excitement

Note: It's important to realize that C- and J-shapes aren't absolute but a continuum: someone tending to the J side might move more towards the C side when pressure strikes.

how to manage them. Without awareness first, we cannot make the butterflies fly in formation.

Body Language and Posture: Taking Command

As we've discussed, when we move into a stressful state we aren't always consciously aware of it. As we come under increasing levels of pressure, our awareness diminishes and our natural reaction is to become more tense and tighter, and as a result our movements become physically smaller.

Before we enter into a stressful situation it is always worth resetting our posture. With a rugby goal kicker, a footballer about to take a penalty, a cricket batsman about to face a delivery and a golfer lining up a shot, I always make it part of a player's pre-shot routine to set their body shape in the 'command' posture and to make themselves as physically big as possible. I advise anyone in a stressful situation to adopt the same approach.

Command posture involves having the shoulders down and packed, with the neck stretched and the chin held in line with the sternum. Despite the title 'command', think less of a military-style standing to attention and more of a trained dancer, upright, lithe and graceful: you are in control of your situation, not standing to the attention of someone or something else.

There are two little experiments you can do in the gym to experience the feel of command posture. The first is to sit on a bench in a *crouched* position and then put a lightly weighted bar – no more than five kilos to start with – across your shoulders. Keeping your legs and hips still, rotate your pillar (the area from the crotch to the top of the head) to the left and then the right. You'll notice how limited and awkward your movement is. Now, with the weights still in place, adopt an upright posture and see how much further you can turn and how much more comfortable supporting the weight becomes.

The second experiment is about awareness. A common piece of apparatus in a gym is the leg-extension machine, on which you sit with your knees bent and your feet hooked behind a padded bar. You extend your legs forward against the resistance you have selected. Once you're warmed up, you should set the resistance so it is difficult for you to move – but not impossible – and attempt to move the bar up. Notice what happens to your pillar: as soon as you apply power through your legs, it naturally straightens to get into a strong and stable position for your legs to work from. This stability and physically strong pillar position – your command posture – allows you to apply your power most effectively.

Next time you enter into a situation you suspect will be stressful, try to take a second before you enter the fray and reset your posture in this manner.

Four-legged Friends

It was late spring a few years ago when the concerned mother of a sixteen-year-old girl approached me. Her daughter was a very talented horse rider, but she had a round-shouldered posture that was costing her points when she competed in the dressage. What made things worse was that, as she became aware of it, she started to feel more pressure in the event, which in turn only made her posture worse. Also, like most sixteen-year-olds, she was spending most evenings hunched over her books or her laptop, revising for her impending exams.

I met the mother and daughter at a café and asked the girl to sit up straight as if she were on a horse and to imagine she had total control of everything in her field of vision. I could see that she was physically capable of command posture, when her mind was set to assuming it, but it wasn't something that came naturally and she didn't have much spare time to practise. I had an idea.

Remembering my previous work with the England polo team, I gave her a figure-8 band to wear over her shoulders and asked her to sit on a stool as if riding a horse again. Perfect posture! I had devised a training regime for her and all she needed was a kitchen timer and a Swiss ball (the type found in gyms). She would train while doing her homework by sitting astride the ball as if on a horse, wearing the figure-8 in command posture. She'd initially do fifteen minutes per session and increase the time by five minutes after every three sessions until she was doing all her revision and homework in command posture. The great result, as her mother explained to me, was that not only did her dressage and posture improve – so also did her concentration on her homework.

Now, this might read like a modern-day equivalent of young ladies at finishing school balancing books on their heads, but the fact is that it worked in this case and it could work for you. You might feel a bit silly sitting at your desk wearing a figure-8 band, but sitting in command posture will have a positive effect not only on your body – no more slumped shoulders and the attendant effects on your neck and back – but also on your state of mind, especially when you're under pressure. You'll feel more alert, more poised. Just fifteen minutes in the morning and again in the afternoon to start, increasing from there (use your phone as a timer), and you'll soon see the benefits. Once you've practised enough for it to become a natural posture, you can discard the figure-8 band. Even if you're on your feet all day, working in a shop or warehouse, the effects are just as beneficial. You could even do it when driving to avoid the classic hunched pose in a traffic jam.

Becoming Big

When I work with goal kickers in rugby on a technical issue and the player is becoming increasingly stressed and frustrated as they struggle to get it right, I will often ask the player to 'become big' with their body and then attempt the kick again. This allows them to reset and take the next kick much more slowly and deliberately, and there is usually a corresponding improvement in the accuracy and control of the kick.

Focusing on 'being big' allows us to take a moment to appreciate what we are doing physically. In a pressure situation, when the natural, often subconscious impulse is for the body to become smaller, crouched and more tense, just like the rush-hour commuters earlier, consciously 'becoming bigger' allows you to stretch out the body and counter these physical inhibitors.

As mentioned earlier, Cristiano Ronaldo's technique as a J-shape kicker gives him the stability to strike the ball so effectively – his upright posture is simply a more powerful physical position. But the advantages of command posture aren't just physical; there are huge mental benefits to be gleaned from adopting it.

Sports commentators regularly talk about body language – 'Their heads have dropped' – demonstrating the link between mental surrender and body language. We see this kind of thing most clearly when there seems to be little chance of winning. But it's a two-way street: just as the mindset of a losing team or competitor can inform body language, so too can the reverse be true. Working on your posture can have a dramatic impact on your state of mind as you prepare to deliver under pressure.

With the England Cricket Performance Squad I have often seen Kevin Shine ask the bowlers to be as 'big as you can be' during the delivery to try to dominate the batsman mentally. Indeed, there is always a contest between the batsman and bowler to control the exchange and body language plays a huge part in this. With each player looking for a chink in the armour of the other, it is often their body language that betrays them, especially when the execution of their shot fails to match their intention, showing that they are not in complete command of the situation.

Under pressure, many athletes from all types of sport consciously set their posture as part of their routine. If you watch tennis player Rafa Nadal before he serves or receives, he has a lengthy routine he goes through before he is mentally and physically ready to play. Jonathan Trott, the former England cricket batsman, was another with quite a pronounced routine – but all players run through a sequence to set themselves. It's particularly noticeable in golf, where players deliberately set their posture and body position before each shot – back straight, neck extended.

Consistently in Command

Command posture isn't only of use as a means to reset your body language before a specific event. It is advisable to maintain this posture throughout whatever you're doing – be it a sales conference or, say, the 2012 BMW PGA Championship at Wentworth.

It was during this tournament – and in the lead-up to it – that I worked with Luke Donald to help him concentrate on maintaining his command posture not only during his shots, but also throughout the entire four rounds. We put particular emphasis on keeping it up between shots, when it is easier to switch off, even for a moment, and fail to adhere to it, in the hope that it would become second nature.

It was a tough week. Luke was bidding to join Nick Faldo and Colin Montgomerie as the only players ever to defend the title successfully, which he did when he pulled away from Justin Rose after the ninth hole in the final round. In an interview afterwards Luke said that his calm on the course was due to the work we had done with his posture:

> It's helped me to really be aware of my posture and how I outwardly project that feeling of positiveness. It helps me send that message to whoever I'm playing with. He [Dave Alred] is certainly always on at me again about keeping the shoulders back and not getting down on myself, staying positive not just mentally but physically and through my body position. So I think I've done a lot better job of it since I've been working with Dave. He's always reminding me.

When I first started working with Luke, in January 2010, one of the first things we worked on together was getting him to show 'inevitability' – imagining that his shot would perfectly match his intention – in his body language *before* the shot, *during* the shot and *after* the shot, while the ball is in the air. Luke quite rightly asked: 'How do I physically show it?'

Think about how you would feel if you *knew* you couldn't fail in performing a particular feat. If the penalty you were about to take was sure to go screaming into the top corner. If the presentation you were about to make was certain to end in a standing ovation. The expressions you'd use to describe the feeling after the event would be things like 'feeling ten feet tall' and 'walking on air', but such statements would almost certainly not reflect your posture prior to the event if you were feeling nervous and anxious.

It's a question of reframing your thoughts to believe that there is an inevitability about what you're going to do: if you *know* you're going to perform brilliantly, then your anxiety before the event will become excitement; your nerves will become anticipation. You can adopt your command posture and assume an air of confidence because you *know* you're going to be successful. It's inevitable. Those who expect you to be exhibiting more signs of tension and apprehension might even construe your manner as arrogance, because a 'normal' person, one without a command posture that shows inevitability and feelings of excitement instead of anxiety, ought to be nervous.

This is the challenge to us: as pressure increases and we naturally become tense and tightened, we need to remember and practise resetting our posture the way top athletes do – not only resetting it before a big occasion, but also maintaining it throughout. And we need to use the confidence this gives us to feel a sense of inevitability about what we're doing – this is going to be a great success, I'm going to feel ten feet tall – so that those feelings of anxiety can start to be welcomed as a natural and expected part of what is to come: a great performance.

The Laws of Speed and Time

We are all familiar with the well-worn vernacular describing foot-ballers who 'appear to have so much time on the ball' or the cricketer who 'sees the ball early' or the snooker player who 'makes the right decisions under pressure', and it's easy to be lulled into the idea that, through their own precocious gifts, such people are naturally blessed. But is this really true?

I regularly conduct management training days in which attendees have to react to pressure and perform both as a member of the team and as a leader. The day is composed of a series of games and activities, with the delegates split into teams and a different person being the leader on each activity. The person in charge is not only responsible for their team's performance, but also needs to coach their team members in the skills and tactics for a contest with the other teams.

The first activity is a simple possession game, not unlike net-ball, with five players per team. The object is to complete as many passes as possible between players on the attacking side, while the defending side's job is to win the ball back. The complicating factor? The defending side can field only three players to the attacking side's five, so that when the attacking side loses posses-sion they have to take two players off – an added challenge for the respective leaders.

Without exception, the start of the game is always absolute chaos. Everyone charges around after the ball, people scream for it to be passed to them, the ball is dropped, passes go astray – it's like watching a game in a school playground played by hyper-active children. The players, excited and pumped on adrenaline, have usually lost track of the score by now and any other infor-mation not relevant to the one thing they're doing: chasing blindly after the ball.

After about sixty to seventy seconds of pure pandemonium, the game is halted. In a simple five-versus-three game like this – a bit like basketball with one team having had two players sent off – the simplest and most effective tactic for the offensive team is to have one player in the middle and one in each of the corners, making it impossible for the defending team to mark everyone so that there is always someone to pass to. Once the players absorb this concept, the game seems to slow down and the players find themselves with more space in which to operate, and consequently more time to make decisions, as long as they are disciplined with their positions on the court.

The next task is an extension of basically the same game but with one important adjustment: no verbal communication is permitted – only eye contact. This, thankfully, makes for a quieter game, but it also leads to a dramatic increase in the players' awareness of the position and spacing of their own team members. By the end of the day, the teams have improved no end from the unrestrained chaos of the start to showing a massive increase in awareness, communication, empathy and control – and eventually posture and composure.

With a bit of understanding and a series of specific practices, every player has left the rushed, time-cramped side of the C–J continuum and is now able to make less hurried and better decisions. In just one day the people on the training course had become markedly better at making effective decisions under pressure. They appeared to have 'more time on the ball', to 'see it all earlier'.

Leading sportspeople, then, aren't just 'naturally' able to appear this way – it is a skill that is the result of practice. While the players at the start of the training day can't even keep track of who's winning, top sports stars are always aware of the score, the time, the position – of their opponent(s) and team mate(s) and the ball – who they might be marking and the tactical options available, and constantly have to make pressured decisions based on combinations of these factors. But they aren't just born with this skill. They have done hours and hours of deliberate practice. The professionals live it – practising all the time they're not playing, while the rest of us no doubt go to work all week and just play in our spare time. Not only that, but they have acquired lots of big-game experience that has enabled them to get better and better. The great news is that, as the training day makes clear, you too can improve.

Keeping in Sequence

Another well-worn sports cliché is of the player whose kick, throw, shot or whatever appears to be effortless. The usual explanation of this particular ability is 'timing'. While this is certainly part of it, there are other factors involved that relate to speed and the ability to be controlled in your movements rather than snatching at them.

If you're partial to a round of golf, or even if you've just unwillingly been dragged along on a company golf day, consider the difference between the smooth action of a professional's swing with a novice trying to hit the ball as hard as he or she possibly can. The novice will use his arms and wrists to try to generate the power – and more often than not will snatch at the ball to some degree. The professional, on the other hand, with a stable lower body, will initially take the club back in a wide arc while turning at the waist and creating a tension in the pillar with his back facing the target. The swing into the ball will start with the legs moving, then the pillar uncoiling as the arms swing down and then the wrists release the club through the ball at well over ninety miles per hour. None of the movements in themselves are quick, but the sum of them produces acceleration and seemingly effortless speed. The difference lies in the sequencing of the individual events that make up the swing.

In 2002 David Rath of the Australian Institute of Sport produced some research on the drop punt in Australian Rules football, in which he produced a precise visual interpretation of the kicking sequencing that produces the fastest speed – a tool that can be applied to other sports such as cricket, football, rugby, throwing the javelin, the shot put . . . the list goes on. Rath believes that the basic principle behind effective sequencing is to use the biggest muscle group to start a movement, then recruit the next biggest and the next before finishing with the smallest.

Imagine you are on a train travelling at 60 mph. You run along the corridor at 8 mph, meaning you are now travelling at 68 mph. As you run, you bowl a ball, during which your hand travels at, say, 40 mph. With your running speed and that of the train involved, the ball is now travelling at 108 mph. Similarly, when a fast bowler in cricket releases the ball, his running speed allied to the speed his pillar turns and then his arm and then the speed his wrist moves forward determines the speed of the ball.

This sequencing can be applied to plenty of things outside sport too. To lift a heavy weight, you bend your knees to recruit your legs, your strongest muscle group, straightening your pillar and only then using your shoulders and arms for support.

For sequencing to have the greatest impact it is essential that each movement in the sequence starts when the preceding movement has reached its maximum speed. To go back to the train, if you were to start running too early and the train was only travelling at 40 mph then, even if you forced some extra effort from yourself and ran at 10 mph and threw the ball at 45 mph, you would only be able to propel the ball at 95 mph. We see this with novices on the cricket pitch and the golf course when they compromise the other elements of the sequence and try to achieve all of the power through the arm(s). Only once you're proficient in the sequence of events can a ball be thrown, kicked or hit with the appearance of so little effort – and so much velocity and control.

However, even an experienced pro can face sequencing issues when the pressure is on. Pressure-induced tightening and shortening of the muscles can, as already discussed, compromise an action a sportsman is making. It changes the movement and stops the sequencing being as efficient as usual. Rather than addressing their sequencing from the ground up, as a performer would usually, someone affected by pressure might concentrate on the extremities – the arms and legs – and as a result become unbalanced, losing both control and accuracy. In effect, they revert to being more like a novice who, as discussed, would try to derive all their power from either their legs – for a kicker – or arms – for a bowler, golfer, tennis player, thrower. A breakdown in sequencing can produce a novice-like behaviour, which causes a player to become very inefficient.

In 2014 I was working with five elite rugby goal kickers: England's Jonny Wilkinson (Toulon) and George Ford (Bath); Ireland's Johnny Sexton (Racing Metro 92 in Paris) and Paddy Jackson (Ulster); and Wales's Rhys Patchell (Cardiff). Each of them was under pressure for different reasons.

When a player under pressure hits the ball hard, there is a tendency to hit at it, rather than through it. I asked the players to visualize a speed 'swoosh' – the trace of the path of the kicker's foot – which started as a green colour and, as it increased in velocity, became yellow and then orange and, finally, in the last twelve inches or so, at its fastest speed, became red. Most importantly, this 'red zone' occurs beyond the ball, not towards the ball. All five players found this image helpful in improving their kicking *through* the ball rather than *to* the ball, which in turn improved their control, power and accuracy. By the end, it looked effortless – but a lot of hard work had gone into getting their sequence just so.

Awareness: The Importance of Being Grounded

When I started working with Luke Donald, I noticed a slight difference between his iron and wood shots; on the latter, he had a tendency to rise up out of his shot – straightening his legs in the process – and I believed it was just a question of awareness. We worked a moment of consciously grounding himself into his pre-shot routine. The process was a simple case of thinking about his feet as being four points on the ground – the heel and toe of each foot – and being aware of these four points as he sank his studs into the earth. This allowed him to have the most stable base possible for his shot and it's very common to see golfers grounding themselves similarly. If nothing else, it's a moment to be consciously aware of the stable platform they're creating – and it's something you could certainly do to centre yourself before a pressure situation of your own.

From Anxiety to Excitement

The C–J concept, although sport based, is a highly useful tool to help you understand and diagnose the potential pressures that can affect people in any activity. My hope is that you will find it a useful checklist to look out for when you try something under pressure – be it your golf swing on the company golf day or your posture and body language when you're sitting at your desk with a pile of work that just won't go away.

The most effective way to learn or improve anything is to apply a method I like to call the 'dentist effect'. Most of us have had an anaesthetic injection before the dentist starts drilling and, afterwards, with our faces feeling like there's a huge gob-stopper wedged in there, and unable to sip a drink without dribbling it down our fronts, have looked in the mirror only to see there is hardly any swelling at all. It just *feels* that way.

To make a change in our method or technique when doing something different, we initially need to exaggerate the change so that it feels substantial and alien. You're changing to a point way beyond where it should be. If you're a goal kicker and you want to improve your follow-through, instead of doing what you usually do and then adding on a follow-through, try jogging through the kick a good two or three yards further than neces-sary; if you're a golfer trying to extend your swing towards the target, try swinging the club and playing further forward through the shot, scuffing the bottom of it on a spot on the grass beyond your front leg – well past where you need it to be; if you do a lot of presentations at work, during which you tend to mumble and look down, try projecting louder than necessary and puffing up your command posture to a point that feels a bit awkward.

If you exaggerate these changes when you practise, then when it comes to doing it for real, when the pressure bites and the muscles tighten, you will have the *feeling* in your memory of running through your kick or extending your swing through the ball or adopting your command posture and loud, projected voice in front of a busy room. It may feel a little different or awkward when you're doing it for real – it should still feel like you're beyond where you're comfortable – but, as with the phantom swelling after your trip to the dentist, it won't appear so to an outside observer. When public speaking, a very good idea is to practise in front of the mirror with your command posture: you may feel self-conscious with your shoulders back and neck re-aligned, but in the mirror you should just appear confident.

By making these changes and feeling the 'dentist effect', you will find yourself moving away from the C-side, the potential physical effects of pressure, towards the J-side of the table, where you will be better able to manage the physical impact of anxiety. As you approach the right-hand side, your feelings of anxiety, the pre-match butterflies, may still express the same symptoms – think of Neil Jenkins throwing up before a match – but they are more likely to be welcomed and expected – to become excitement. The excitement that Jack Nicklaus would do anything to experi-ence again in the early round of majors – the excitement that is a high-octane fuel for a great performance.

Anxiety isn't a weakness. We need to reframe the way we feel about it and understand that adrenaline production is a natural bodily response to an impending pressured event. This is our famous 'fight-or-flight' mechanism, evolution's gift from our ances-tors for whom it was a vital response to danger, but which today is applied to many modern situations we face that aren't literally dangerous. So, through practice and self-awareness we can move towards the right side of the C–J table and take some degree of control over our feelings of anxiety. With practice, we can manage these effects of pressure and turn them into excitement, something to be welcomed. And if we can do this, then we can better begin to perform to our potential under pressure. Our anticipation of a highly pressured event should not be one of dread, it should be more like a child's excitement on Christmas Eve.

Principle 1: Anxiety

Anxiety should be regarded as high-octane fuel for elite performance and as a normal reaction to a pressured environment. The skill is managing it so we can perform to our limits under pressure.

If anxiety is perceived as a weakness, it will have a detrimental impact on our ability to perform under pressure.

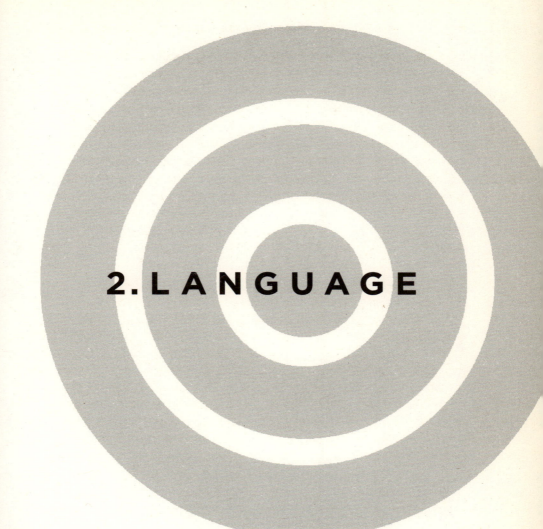

2.LANGUAGE

2.

The Ultimate Performance-Enhancing Drug

Words are, of course, the most powerful drug used by mankind.
Rudyard Kipling

A new performance drug is now being used in the development of England's elite cricket players and coaches. It has been said that it is the most powerful drug known to mankind. The performance edges that can be achieved from skilful and consistent use of this drug include: increasing self-esteem, creating a dramatic boost in confidence, reframing and transforming meaning, and changes in behaviours and attitudes. The 'health warning' that accompanies this powerful drug is the fact that it is in abundance, has no monetary cost, and many people simply are not aware of its existence or power! Therefore, it can easily be misused and is often abused.

Most people are unaware of its existence. Individuals often suffer untold damage without knowing what or who the culprit is until it's too late, and this makes it even more dangerous. Even after the cause (careless use) and effect have been recognized and understood, it can potentially take years to repair the damage. Sadly, in many cases the individual never fully recovers from its misuse, and it can destroy self-esteem, shatter confidence and severely limit performance potential, particularly when the performance involves making decisions.

I wrote this in the summer of 2009 for the ECB's coaching magazine *On the Up*, when I became heavily involved with their Level

Four Cricket Coaching Programme, under the headline: 'The Most Powerful Performance Drug Now Being Used in English Cricket'. The drug is language, and the irony is that the media – particularly the headline writers – are among its greatest manipulators and misusers.

The impact of language is far-reaching and its effects can be felt, often subconsciously, throughout any situation we face involving pressure. It can be damaging and disruptive to performance or it can dramatically improve it, but, sadly, the skill of using language effectively is largely ignored in the world of sports coaching.

Language is of vital importance to the Pressure Principle, in that it is crucial to the effectiveness of the other seven components. We have already discussed anxiety and the need to transform its negative impact into excitement, and later chapters will examine the importance of types and methods of learning and practice, of behaviour and environment. But what informs all of these is the language that goes into them, that reinforces them and allows you to tap into your subconscious effectively for a great performance. If the other chapters fuel the engine of your great performance, language is the oil to keep things running smoothly. And, as anyone who has failed to keep the oil in their car topped up knows, the engine just won't work without it.

One industry where the importance of language is certainly not lost on anyone is advertising. Large businesses are prepared to pump millions into advertising their products and huge campaigns often hinge on one carefully crafted slogan. Advertisers use persuasive language, emotive words and all sorts of linguistic tricks to attract us, particularly on a subconscious level; after all, which of us doesn't imagine themselves to be immune to the power of advertising? Consider the groundbreaking 'Think small' VW Beetle adverts of the 1950s, Apple's 'Think different' or any number of equally memorable slogans ('For mash get Smash'; 'Anytime, anyplace, anywhere – that's Martini'). Some are cute and catchy, but something beyond that is going on. This language is geared to appeal to us, to provoke a reaction and response and, ultimately, to change our behaviour. Sound familiar? It's really not that different from what we aim to achieve when coaching or managing people.

How, then, can we gauge the impact of language when it operates on such a subconscious level? In his book *Blink*, Malcolm Gladwell describes an experiment by John Bargh, an American psychologist, in which he looked at the subconscious influence of language and its impact on attitude and behaviour. He gave two groups of New York students a different set of scrambled-sentence tests – a series of mixed-up sentences which have to be reordered to make proper sentences. The first group had sentences containing words such as 'aggressively', 'bold', 'rude', 'bother', 'disturb', 'intrude' and 'infringe' scattered throughout. The other group received words such as 'respect', 'considerate', 'appreciate', 'patiently', 'yield', 'polite' and 'courteous'. In neither case was the bias so obvious as to make the students conscious of what was happening, as that would negate the power of the experiment. After completing the test, the students were asked to hand them in at an office, where the intended recipient was deliberately engaged in deep conversation with someone else, keeping the students waiting.

The aim of the experiment was to see whether the two groups reacted differently to the delay. Bargh expected the 'aggressively primed' students to interrupt slightly earlier than the passive group; in fact, the difference was much more pronounced: the first group interrupted on average after five minutes, but 82 per cent of the second group didn't interrupt at all.

Reframing

I believe that language can influence and create an attitude and can help you reframe your perception of what you experience. Take a very simple example: are you a glass-half-full or half-empty type? The common attitude is that to see the glass half full is more positive than seeing it half empty. To put it another way, half full is what you have got and half empty is what you are missing. Reframing is simply taking a situation and changing the way you look at it, by changing the frame of reference around a statement without changing the facts. By using different words you can change the meaning and, as a result, change how you feel.

The ability to reframe a situation will support your effort to feel excited rather than anxious. Here are some simple examples of how to use language to change the way you see things:

Standing in the tunnel with the rest of your team, just before running out in front of a big crowd:

Anxious: Oh, dear. I hope I don't make a mistake and have the crowd turn on me.

Excited: What a buzz – there isn't one person out there who doesn't wish they were in my shoes right now.

You are in the office corridor, waiting to make a presentation to a client:

Anxious: I hate doing these things – if I mess up, what on earth will they think of me?

Excited: They don't know me. I will have impressive posture and look them straight in the eyes – they're people too, just like me.

Going into an appraisal with your manager:

Anxious: I hope I don't get any criticism; I hate it when they pick holes in my work.

Excited: It will be great to hear how I can still improve. I have tried to cover everything, but I may well have missed out something.

Your choice of language gives you the ability to reframe your situation or, to be more precise, reframe your perception of the situation. This and your command posture are the fundamental tools that will enable you to shift from a state of anxiety (the C-shape column) to excitement (the J-shape column).

Maddening Men: The Misuse of Language

Effective use of language can influence and inform an attitude of performance improvement, and a collective attitude in turn creates a culture – be it among a sports squad, a team in your business or even in the family. For a golfer, this culture must be created by his team around him – his coaches, caddie and management. I have been really fortunate when working with Padraig Harrington and Luke Donald that they had superb caddies – Ronan Flood and John McLaren, respectively. We worked as a unit to produce a team culture and help each other find the right buttons to push.

While it is easy to see how a collective attitude can create a culture within a group, in my experience it is harder to appreciate just how important language skills are in creating the right attitude. Language can be a tool both for good and ill, and it's often easier to be aware of its misuse than it is to see how effective it can be, especially in the sporting world. Some of the most passionately delivered misuses of language are bellowed from the touchline at the weekend in all levels of sport – be it a Premier League football fixture or a youth game of cricket on the village green:

'No missed tackles!'

'No dropped passes!'

'Don't lose concentration!'

'Make sure you don't get out too early!'

'Don't bowl short of a length!'

'Don't drop the crosses coming over!'

'Don't let him run round you!'

These are all, of course, examples of the 'Don't Miss!' mindset from Chapter 1, in which the power of thinking about what *not* to do pollutes the brain with the idea of missing, filling it with that which you want to avoid. If you have a coach or a manager telling you what *not* to do, they are planting the idea in the exact same way. Language is so powerful that even a hint of what you are trying to avoid can be fateful, as demonstrated by John Bargh's experiment. Even when the words are being used as something *not* to do, our brains take it on board and we're subconsciously drawn to this very thing. As a well-worn example, how about I ask you not to think of a purple elephant. OK? What are you not thinking about now?

When someone on the golf course tells you, 'This is a simple par three, but you don't want to go right because there's water there and you don't want to go in the water,' it is said helpfully. But guess where the first shot goes? The water becomes a magnet to the ball, as your brain is full of thoughts of what not to do and what to avoid.

Conscious thought of what you *want* to do, supported by basic mental cues on how physically to do it – the process – is a much more effective and productive mindset. Where language becomes important is in communicating – whether as a manager, coach or caddie – in a way that highlights the effective aspects of the process, as in Table 2.

A lot of coaches might say, 'But the players know what I mean.' I don't doubt for a second that they do, but it's more about the mental image you're projecting through your choice of words. If you say 'No dropped passes', the player's brain will conjure up an image of a dropped pass and then adjust to see it as something not to do. Wouldn't it make sense to project only the image of what you want to achieve into the player's mind?

Let's imagine an advertising creative, Alastair. He has been briefed to produce something brilliantly innovative and original, but the deadline is looming and he's drawn a blank. The pressure is really on and he's summoned to his manager's office for what he hopes will be an inspirational pep talk. Instead, he gets,

Table 2 Turning negative statements into effective ones

Negative	Effective
No missed tackles! (rugby)	See right into the player's navel and get as low as his waist and run through his stomach.
No dropped passes! (rugby, netball, basketball)	Hands out to meet every ball early. When you are passing, see the ball to the target.
Don't lose concentration!	Commentate on what you see and what you are doing in the game, always keep talking.
Don't bowl short of a length!	Make sure you really see the smallest precise target on the pitch and keep it in your mind's eye.
Make sure you don't get out too early! (cricket)	Stay nice and big and dominate each ball, keeping your head still.
Don't drop the crosses coming in! (football goalkeeper)	Watch the ball all the way into your hands – up to the point that you can read the logo on the ball.
Don't let an opponent run round you!	Stay on your opponent's right side and force them to the touchline.

'I want something on my desk by 5 p.m. – *and make sure it's nothing like our biggest rival's campaign for a similar brand!*' Alastair, the adrenaline pumping, returns to his desk. *Can you rush creativity?* he thinks, rather preciously. And then he sits down and thinks some more about the idea. With the clock ticking and his stress levels rising, all Alastair can see in his mind is the rival's ad – what he *shouldn't* be doing. He comes up with some hurried ideas, but then starts to realize that every one is a reaction to the rival idea – using what he's *not* to do as a starting point. He tears them all up and starts again, but the clock is ticking . . . If only his manager hadn't planted that seed.

When I was coaching at Bath RFC, the captain, Stuart Hooper, would give a pep talk to his teammates just before the team took to the field. From my vantage point in the corner, I would listen to a passionate speech peppered with colourful expletives and plenty of what not to do: *No missed tackles! No dropped passes! No regrets!*

After sitting through a couple of his pre-match fire-ups I took Stuart – who possesses an outstanding work ethic and a real willingness to learn and improve – for a coffee and a chat. I pressed upon him the importance of painting pictures with language so that the players were left in no doubt as to what they were supposed to be doing, without clouding their minds with negatives that would affect their thought process when the pressure was on.

Stuart made a real effort to take my advice on board. His use of language improved markedly during the next few matches and we continued to concentrate on this aspect of his game leadership. As a result of our work together, his own performance levels on the field improved dramatically, as he was spending a considerable amount of time thinking through exactly what he was saying – always in a 'how to' form.

'How to' language is a vital component when examining performance and looking at opportunities to improve. Rather than putting the responsibility on the players to work out what to *do* from what they have been told to *avoid*, it is more effective to get straight to the point and have them work through exactly what it is that they need to achieve. The 'how to' in each situation will vary – it could be a slight adjustment to the way a player strikes the ball or a different way to make a point during a sales meeting – but the important thing is that it will be giving someone the opportunity to do something well rather than not to do something badly. 'How to' language, of course, doesn't mean explaining the entire activity step by step; rather it should comprise little cues to remind the player of stages in the process, such as, 'That was a great hit and *your posture was upright and powerful during impact.*'

Adopting 'how to' language isn't easy, particularly if we have for so long been unknowingly careless – and coaches or managers are also susceptible to the effects of pressure, which can inhibit our ability to use language as effectively as we might like. It's often easy to forget that those in charge are just as open as we are to anxiety and problems caused by pressure, and their sometimes unhelpful instructions are as a result of this.

Let's consider some of these overused generalities which are often delivered with such feeling that they sound impressive . . . until you look at what they actually mean. Ask yourself how precisely these nuggets of wisdom might inspire anyone to improve their performance. I'm sure you can come up with many similar examples from your own experience.

Get stuck in! One of the most popular generalities in sport and business, which is often used when the coach or manager thinks effort is lacking. The question is, once given this instruction, what exactly should be done to improve performance? Go and pick a fight?

How about encouragingly shouting the main process that will help the players improve their performance instead? To a defender in football, it could be: 'Stay goal side and force him to the touchline.' On the rugby pitch it could be: 'Hands out – meet the ball early!' In the office, it could be: 'You're doing great. If we concentrate on this aspect we could nail this by the end of the day!'

Keep your eye on the ball! This is a classic. In his book *The Inner Game of Tennis*, Timothy Gallwey gives a great example. Imagine you're playing a game of tennis and it's just not your day: the net feels much higher than normal and the court on the other side of it seems much smaller than your side. You swing and miss at a couple of shots and then you receive that priceless piece of advice: 'Keep your eye on the ball.' Now, with renewed vigour you really watch the ball as your opponent serves. You watch it as they toss it up, you watch it as they swing their racket towards it and it comes off the strings like a laser, you watch it as it bounces in your service box and comes towards you – and you watch it as you take your racquet back and swing at it and miss. You are still watching it as it pings off the chain-link fence behind you. What went wrong? You kept your eye on the ball. You did exactly *what* you were told, but there was no 'how to' in there. Instead, you could say something like, 'See the logo on the ball as your racket hits it,' a much more precise instruction concentrating on a specific part of the process.

Switch on! Let's really focus! An emotive cry for increased mental application – but what exactly does it mean? How about, instead, 'Commentate on what you see and do – always keep talking!' Again, there's a process to focus on here, a *how* to switch on and focus, and this match dialogue you open up will help keep you ahead of the game.

A good rule with instructions is 'if you can't see it, don't say it'. If the intention is to get someone to focus and correct a specific part of their process, then say so. An example might be 'Direct every pass towards the hands.' So long as the 'how to' has been perfected through the techniques described later in the book, the language of any instruction can be appropriately framed to tap into this precisely. When vague generalities are used, people are too often left wondering exactly what they are supposed to do.

Never Say Never Again

Tied in with such sweeping generalities are universal statements, which can be just as unhelpful – and so often deliver a destructive message.

I once had a golf lesson from a coach who was an ex-European Tour professional. There was no question that he knew all about the technical side of things – the swing and the mechanics involved. He changed my grip slightly, which felt awkward at first when I took my club back but, during the downswing, I felt a fresh sensation of freedom towards the ball. After a few mishits, I started to strike the ball really well. An improvement already – fantastic!

He videoed my swing and we watched the footage back, with my swing on one side of the screen and one of the greatest players ever to play the game – Tiger Woods – on the other. He proceeded to explain at some length why, no matter how many balls I went on to hit, I would *never* have a swing like Tiger's: I had the wrong body shape, was flexible in the wrong places – on and on he went.

It was hardly news to me that my swing was nothing like that of a fourteen-time major winner, but the universal absolutes with which the message was delivered would have been enough to destroy the confidence of any budding player looking to improve. 'You will *never* have a swing like that – it's impossible with your body and the way it works.'

How is dealing in such unequivocal, universal statements like that going to foster a mindset for anyone to dedicate themselves to improving? With a greater awareness of the impact of his language he could have given me some information that would have encouraged me to continue practising and even return for more lessons. What a difference a statement like this would have made: 'Tiger is able to get in these positions because he has played golf all his life and works very hard on his mobility. While I don't expect you to replicate him exactly, if you can move further towards these kinds of positions it will improve your swing path, ball striking and direction.'

When a player I'm coaching uses universals – *always*, *never* – I *always* pick them up on it. It's vital to make them aware of exactly what they've said, what it means and how, if left unchecked, it can sap confidence. Never means not *ever*; always means *every* time. These words are almost always the precursors to self-criticism. Here are a few examples:

I always mess these putts up. Does that mean you have missed every single putt you have ever attempted? Golf, perhaps more than most sports, has the ability to engender a fear of missing which can become catastrophic. As we've already discussed, these negative thoughts of avoiding missing can pollute our thinking, which, when coupled with an inability to recall an instance of success, hardly makes for the best mindset when trying to nail the putt. Of course, it's not just golf where this occurs. It could be 'I always mess job interviews up' or 'I always mess up first dates' – anything. The point is that the universal statement – the always – isn't allowing for the instances where there has been success and is closing the door on us latching on to a more positive instance to inspire confidence. Clearer thinking about the process, about how best to prepare for the interview and behave during it, would be much easier without the dramatic universal *always*.

I could do nothing right today – I was awful. Nothing at all? No matter how badly a day has gone, there is always something good to look back on. Say you worked in a bookshop. You might have been late for work because you had trouble getting the kids to school that morning, which resulted in a ticking off from your manager. You were tired all day and things were busy, with a couple of rude, impatient customers, before you picked the kids up and chaos ensued once again at home. You did nothing right? You're forgetting the smile on your children's faces when they greeted you at the school gates, the old man you helped order the book he was desperate to get hold of and the amusing chat you had with one of your colleagues on your tea break. It only takes one or two bad incidents to condition our thinking to deal in this kind of negative universal – our brains are negatively biased, after all, as we'll see later – but the truth is that usually it's not all bad.

Returning to golf, I watched an interview with Lee Westwood, in which he was responding to the loaded jibe from a reporter along the lines of: 'Lee, aren't you disappointed in how you played today with that treble [bogey] on the seventeenth?'

Lee's reply was great, as he said he was actually pleased with the way he'd played that day, as he was struggling with his hip release in his swing but still managed to get the ball round really well and shoot a good score of sixty-eight.

This illustrates Lee's ability to compartmentalize his game and, while recognizing that he had one issue, be able to see the good that he was doing. It is such a vital skill in any discipline, and any walk of life, to be able to analyse and separate different aspects of performance, the good and the bad, instead of to catastrophize instinctively and tell yourself it was all bad.

He never gets these kicks on the right-hand side about 15 metres from touch. This was how a reporter criticized Johnny Sexton's goal kicking after he'd missed a kick from that position when Ireland played New Zealand in Dublin at the end of 2013. A successful kick would have put Ireland in a position to make history by beating the All Blacks for the first time.

I was working with Johnny during the summer of 2014. When his club side, Racing Metro, played Clermont in the French top tier, Johnny had to take a crucial kick on the right-hand side, about ten yards from touch. He never gets these, does he? I've never seen a kick hit with such venom – married with a complete control – and it sailed between the posts.

When I'm working with a player and it's getting frustrating and difficult, slowing down and starting again, players often lose their composure and vent their frustration: 'I will *never* get this!' You will have experienced this yourself when learning a new skill or trying to get the hang of something like riding a bike as a child. You'll fall off, get going again, fall off, really get going and then . . . fall off again. *'I'll never get this!'*

But my response is simply to say: 'You haven't got it *yet*.' Reset and start again, keep going and you will get better. We don't deal in universals for the simple reason that we all have the capacity to learn a new skill or improve an existing one – riding a bike, working on your kicking game, getting better at interviews. These are not absolutes – it's only the language we choose that makes them so.

Puzzle Mentality

One facet of performance universal statements can affect most is decision-making. Making effective decisions under pressure is one of the greatest skills anyone can master, as it demonstrates an ability to manage convincingly the effects of pressure and remain mentally sharp, and coaching this skill both in business and on the sports field is a major part of my work with pressure.

All too often, however, the language used by coaches is just too absolute. It's either the 'right' option or the 'wrong' one. This can lead to those being coached adopting a 'puzzle mentality', whereby they search for the one 'correct' option; whereas in reality there are usually lots of options, each with their own advantages and drawbacks.

When I was working towards my masters degree at Bristol University, I looked at the importance of developing problem-solving skills by thinking through and discussing the options available, rather than the simple right-or-wrong mentality. If a teacher, manager or coach is pushing for the 'right' decision, it can lead to the use of guesswork rather than initiative, the student simply saying what he or she thinks the teacher wants to hear.

It is far more important that people use their initiative to make decisions, with any debriefing being geared not towards the 'correctness' of the decision – an absolute – but towards its efficacy. Was a more effective alternative available? What were the other options? There should be no 'wrong' decision – a wrong decision is a guess without reason. By changing the language from absolutes to a continuum of effectiveness we can inspire confidence in people to take more responsibility for their decisions and feel more willing to use their initiative.

'That's Great, Everyone'

The final use of universal absolutes will be familiar to anyone who has been through a training session or a meeting where, at the end of it, the person leading the meeting declares: 'That was great – well done, everyone.' At the other end of the spectrum, which occurs more frequently in the sporting world than the business world, the coach might declare: 'That was rubbish. You should all be ashamed of yourselves.' Neither statement is likely to be entirely accurate.

The first suggests that everything about the meeting, and everyone in it, was of a great standard and it couldn't have gone smoother. But your experience might have been one of sitting through an interminable Monday-morning meeting, constantly watching the clock and desperate for it to end, or perhaps you were daydreaming about going out for dinner or to the pub after work. In that case, you certainly won't have put in a 'great' performance.

In my experience in sport, it is very unlikely that every player will have performed as well during a training session as such a comment would suggest. A 'great session' implies that all players performed to their best, with little room for improvement. Were all the players' techniques faultless? Were you watching every individual all the time? Of course, sometimes after a lacklustre session or meeting it's important to gee people up, and some morale-boosting words can be an effective placebo, but more often than not the nondescript universal 'great' leads only to complacency. It creates a false sense of achievement. Do this enough and you end up with players who are comfortable with their current level of skill and performance and satisfied with being just good enough. Some coaches, after a chastening defeat on match day, are unable to understand what has gone wrong because they've had such a 'great' series of sessions on the training pitch that week.

While you may feel guilty, having clock-watched or thought of that cold beer waiting for you after work, 'That's great, everyone!' lets you off the hook. It reinforces the idea that you don't have to bring your A-game to the meeting and that it's OK to sleepwalk right through it.

In many people's workplaces, interminable meetings go on regularly, with a vague sense that they are achieving something, even if no one is quite sure what. Wouldn't it be more productive to question why you and your colleagues sit around for hours listening to largely irrelevant information? Do we need to discuss every department in every meeting? Would a series of smaller meetings be more effective?

Sports coaches are usually more frank about bad sessions and dishing out criticism compared to the business world. Using precise language improves the level of awareness and quality of feedback and results. Leaving players or team members in no doubt that their effort is recognized but that more is expected where necessary is paramount. In rugby, the day before the second England vs South Africa Test in Bloemfontein in 2000, we had one of our worst training sessions in terms of mistakes. There was no labelling a session like that with the universal tag 'great': Martin Johnson, the captain, stated at the end of it, 'Well, that couldn't be any fucking worse!' But in fact it was an effective session in terms of feedback and preparation for an unpredictable event like a rugby international. On match day we beat the Springboks on their own patch for the first time in six years.

It's Not (Just) What You Say
But the Way that You Say It

Words alone, no matter how precise and effective they are at painting the right mental picture for the recipient, are not always enough to get the message across. It is frequently claimed that most communication is non-verbal, not least by those quoting psychologist Albert Mehrabian, who devised the 7 per cent rule which states that words account for only 7 per cent of communication, while 55 per cent is via body language and 38 per cent is through voice tone. In fact, Mehrabian's work was geared towards expressing attitudes and feelings and has been regularly quoted out of context, questioned and criticized, so we can hardly claim that 93 per cent of *all* communication is non-verbal.

However, it is unarguably true that, to a greater or lesser extent, body language, tone of voice and other non-verbal indicators do matter when communicating. If the verbal message does not tally with the non-verbal, then its effectiveness can be destroyed. To give an extreme example, if you were to tell someone their work on a project was excellent while you were wearing a smirk and avoiding eye contact, they would be unlikely to believe you and would probably be offended. Similarly, an exhortation to 'Be more precise and show more enthusiasm on the pitch!' delivered by someone with a slovenly, untidy appearance, poor posture and a lackadaisical manner – all completely at odds with the verbal message – is unlikely to be taken seriously.

Body language, which is important in helping us make the transition from anxiety to excitement, is equally important when a coach, teacher or manager delivers a message. It's not called body *language* for nothing. It must support the tone of voice and the words being uttered to produce a unified, clear communication. It is vital that there is consistency between the message and the manner of its delivery, otherwise its effectiveness will be diminished, or even lost altogether.

Tone of voice – 38 per cent of communication according to Mehrabian's study – is clearly also vitally important and the message must be delivered with the objective in mind. While I was working in French rugby I was present at a meeting in which a coach was reviewing the previous game on video, pausing the tape whenever there was a mistake and berating the player responsible. At times, such as when the coach was pointing out an attempted tackle that lacked the requisite intensity, the passionate dressing down he delivered was not only well deserved but also correctly communicated – aggressively, to fire the player up so that next time they knew to bring more aggression to their tackling.

However, a kicker missing a penalty then received exactly the same barrage of abuse. While aggression is helpful when tackling, it does not assist a player kicking at goal one iota. Being too aggressive, with the attendant surge of adrenaline, diminishes the control that is essential in place kicking. In this instance the criticism could have been justified, but the delivery was counterproductive. Far better to pass judgement calmly and matter-of-factly, echoing the precise nature of goal kicking rather than the bear-pit mentality required when tackling a sixteen-stone forward.

I have also been present at some inspirational team meetings over the last twenty years. Right up among them would be Jim Telfer's address to the British Lions prior to playing Orange Free State in South Africa in 1997 and Ian McGeechan's to the team prior to the series-clinching Test in Durban a few days later. They were the perfect marriage of the three aspects of communication – words, body language and tone of voice – which felt like much more than the sum of their parts: the posture; the passion; the explicit desire; eye contact; enthusiasm. It was incredible just being in those rooms – and, as the results went on to prove, they were highly effective pieces of oratory.

It is through unifying the verbal and the non-verbal – in marrying these two facets so that they deliver the same message – that we can produce clear and, when the occasion demands it, inspirational communication. If you say the right thing to your employees but you deliver it with soppy negativity, then your message will be partly or entirely lost. You need to have consistency in your intentions and your delivery, so that your choice of words, the tone of your voice and your body language are working together to produce clear, unified instruction. Only then will you be able to convey your message as effectively as you would like.

Of course, consistency alone isn't enough if the message is wrong in the first place, and choosing the right message is the crux of using effective, powerful language.

When Too Much Positive Can Become a Negative

So far we have chiefly covered the misuse of language, the what not to do, but language used skilfully can be a powerful performance enhancer. Just as the advertising industry uses precise, powerful language to try to change the way we look at things and our behaviour as consumers, so managers, coaches and teachers should be doing the same to affect the attitude and behaviour of those we work with.

The most natural form of language use that springs to mind is 'Be positive!' But being positive in our language use simply isn't enough – it's too weak. Positivity alone lends itself to too many sweeping generalities and universal statements – 'That's great/fantastic/excellent, well done!' – without providing a platform for improvement. Of course, positivity has its place, and achieving targets and the like should be met with positive language, but I prefer to think of effective language use as being *productive* language:

NEGATIVE	POSITIVE	PRODUCTIVE
(What to avoid)	(Nice, but where's the direction?)	(Specific how to)

Where this 'positive' language becomes particularly problematic is when its recipient can see straight through it. Too many hollow, sweeping statements are given out by managers and coaches under the assumption that negative is bad so positive must be good. 'Positive' is a hugely overused word in our vocabulary and it is too often used to disguise a lack of precision or specific direction. How can it be positive language when it's failing to have a positive effect?

I once stood watching a US PGA golf coach whose stock positive phrase was 'Nice swing,' or 'Nice job,' followed by the player's name. My issue with this was that he wasn't stating why it was a nice swing and consequently what the player would need to do to repeat it. When I watched another coach with a European Tour player, he gave out the same – 'Nice swing' – but when I spoke to the player afterwards, he was livid, saying he was 'swinging like shit' and was becoming increasingly irritated and distracted by the coach's empty positivity.

So, what kind of language might induce a more useful and performance-improving state? Here is an example from rugby goal kicking:

The first step is to have a powerful 'how to' statement, like the 'how to' language we discussed earlier:

Big posture, crush the inside quarter [of the ball] and accelerate over the far peg [on the tee].

The second step is to say vividly what happens when it's right:

See the ball cannon off your foot up the line to the middle of the posts. Make this mental rehearsal as vivid as possible; feel the ball off the foot, see the exact flight of the ball splitting the uprights with a slow controlled spin.

Having practised within a structured regime, the player *knows* what a good kick is – how it feels to match their intentions exactly.

The third step should conjure up the requisite emotional state:

Show with your body language [posture] that you expect to match your intention exactly. Adopt a state of controlled aggressive inevitability towards your intention.

The correct emotional state for a task varies depending on the activity – kicking at goal in rugby would require a mindset different from, say, taking the microphone at a karaoke night when your natural instinct is to hide in the corner – and it is the precise use of language that will best conjure up the right feeling. As anyone in advertising knows, emotive words such as 'explode', 'coiled', 'crush', 'spring', 'aggressive', 'controlled', 'icy' or 'flow' can all help to develop the most productive mindset for pressure situations.

Effective language enables us to zone in on precise thoughts, feelings and actions that can help us match our intentions and be successful when the pressure is on. It's not just what you do, but how you need to feel to be able to do it; if we want to change our actions then we need to change the thoughts and feelings that produce them.

You might be sitting in the corner at a works karaoke night – to you, the worst kind of team bonding imaginable. You're waiting for the ground to swallow you up, when your boss hands you the mic and says, 'It's your turn. Get up there and sing.' This is hardly the kind of call to arms that's going to have you getting up to belt out a pop classic. But suppose instead your boss had called you over to the stage, thrust the mic into your hands and ordered you to, 'Get up there and own that song – I want to see you smash it!' That's the kind of powerful, emotive language that will have you either running for the exit door or have you bounding up to the stage ready to bring the house down.

Similarly, a simple goal-kicking coaching instruction – 'When you kick, do your best to hit the ball on the inside quarter panel' – is technically correct, but 'Try to dominate the ball and crush the inside quarter' is more likely to produce the desired result.

The words 'dominate' and 'crush' imply that you must get your body over the ball and hit down on it. It's a shorter, more potent and more effective statement; in the case of language, less is usually more.

You Talking to Me?

Thinking things through beforehand, consciously and intentionally in more productive terms, much like I described Stuart Hooper doing earlier before he addressed his teammates, can help stimulate what I call 'self-talk'. Self-talk can affect thoughts, which in turn can determine your feelings about something and ultimately have an impact on behaviour.

While I'm not suggesting you lock yourself in an empty room and start talking to yourself, I do believe that conscious, intentional and productive thinking – the self-talk – can help to effectively 'brainwash' you into changing your thinking so that you know exactly what you are going to do and how you are going to do it.

The powerful language cues we use when learning new skills or thinking things through in advance can be cemented in the mind through practice, repetition or, as for Stuart Hooper, through repetition to others (his teammates), so that they can be easily recalled in a tense, pressured environment such as a rugby match.

A really good example of self-talk is used by driving instructors. Anyone who has learned to drive will never forget the phrase 'Mirror, signal, manoeuvre' – three words that contain a wealth of information for the learner driver. Mirror – to check your mirrors for any vehicles or pedestrians in the way – signal – doing this in good time to make your intentions clear to other road users – and the manoeuvre – safely using the steering, speed and position of the car to enter a traffic stream, navigate a roundabout or junction or change lanes on a motorway. While this may become second nature to experienced drivers, for learners it can be an invaluable aid in pressure situations such as driving on a busy road or, indeed, taking a driving test. That 'Mirror, signal, manoeuvre' self-talk is their cue to carry out the sequence they've practised many times and lends some order and clarity to their minds when the pressure bites – all through three simple words.

We created a simple self-talk phrase for the players leading up to the Rugby World Cup in 2003: 'Crossbar, touchlines, crossbar.' Every time a player turned to face the opposition the idea was that he would scan the crossbar joining posts at the end of the field; the touchline on one side of the pitch, then the other touchline, and then crossbar again. Why would this help? Under pressure, players are often drawn into looking at the opposition players rather than the space on the field. When a player looks to the touchline, he will see the space outside the last man, which is particularly relevant when teams condense to only using half the width of the pitch. A simple self-talk of 'Crossbar, touchlines, crossbar' prompts the player to run through a routine to help them identify space on the pitch.

Affirmative Action

There is no substitute for powerful, productive 'how to' language, both as a means of coaching and in self-talk, to help foster the right mindset for performing under pressure. Language is the oil in the engine of a great performance and it directly affects every other aspect of the Pressure Principle. Perhaps the most important use of language, the distillation of its power, comes in its smallest bundle: the affirmation.

Self-help gurus use them and advertising companies certainly use them; affirmations are short, potent statements that, despite their size, are able to unlock a great deal of meaning – literal, emotional and physical – from our minds. A handful of words with all that power.

It is a similar principle that I try to apply in writing affirmations for the players I coach: precise, tailored and personal notes, produced after I have worked with them for a while and have a grasp of what makes them tick and what they need to do to improve. It is imperative that the language is productive and not merely glibly positive.

I tend to produce two types of affirmations for players: one for a specific event, match or round, designed to evoke the confidence that a successful outcome will be secured if certain processes are followed; the other focuses on a more general approach to improve all-round performance and attitude in training, practice and performance.

I put the following together for a golfer who was determined to improve but needed to be tougher in his practice and more aggressive in his play:

- *I am one of the most committed, skilful and mentally tough golfers in the world.*
- *My biggest challenge is to play MY game whatever the environment.*
- *I am most effective when my mindset is evil; I display inevitability and dominate each shot.*
- *I relish pressure and always long for those great occasions.*
- *I am driven to continually work in the uncomfortable zone.*
- *I know there are no limits at the margin of every component of my game and preparation.*
- *My time has come.*

The first point is a factual statement of who he is without slipping into 'absolute' language. One of the best is a fact, while being *the* best – well, there can be only one. The next parts ensure that his main obstacle, which we'd identified together, is covered and then identify the keys to his most effective mindset. The aim is to conclude that, if he adheres to the process and practice, he will improve. He went on to become the world's number one golfer.

Here is another general one, which I put together for a member of the victorious British and Irish Lions squad during their tour of Australia in 2013. He was a right-footed kicker already improving and getting tougher on himself in training, practising right at the edge of his ability and working tirelessly on his left-footed kicking:

- *I am a committed, brave and skilful player, with the potential to dominate international rugby. I am now on the crest of a wave and I am not going to let this momentum get away from me.*
- *My commitment to improving every component of my game has no limits. I understand angst and working in the ugly, uncomfortable areas, and that meeting that ugly area head-on will separate me from those who want to stay comfortable – comfort does not make you better.*
- *I know it is tough being totally focused on my performance, but it is that which makes me different and as a result better in the long run, and will continue to enhance my ability to perform under pressure.*
- *There will always be distractions and doubters but they can never penetrate my secure performance bubble. I know I will just keep getting better. There are no limits at the margin of everything I do.*

The structure is similar to that of the golfer's. Firstly, there is a statement about himself and his situation. He then reaffirms his commitment to training in the ugly zone (see Chapter 3) and why it is essential for him, acknowledging that it will be tough but eventually rewarding through improved performances.

Here is another affirmation for an international rugby player who is a forward and wanted to improve several areas of his game. This one is short and to the point:

- *I have accepted my biggest challenge – getting ugly with the parts of the game that will enable me to become the complete world-class player.*

- *I am a function of the team – decisive, destructive, aggressive and becoming more reliable.*
- *I must convey my enthusiasm and commitment to the cause by showing urgency, alertness and total involvement.*

Again, it is the same basic structure with the challenge inter-woven within the statements. It's not a case of just writing a few sentences and then hoping everything will be fine; it's writing them, reading them, keeping them somewhere special (the golfer had his in his scorecard holder) and living them. There will always be conditions to improvement and those are the things that the player has to change. Feeling good about yourself is a good framework to start with, then you have to commit. When I work with someone over a period of time, we regularly review their affirmations together and update when necessary to keep the challenge fresh.

The second type of affirmation, to promote and support the right mindset prior to the event, is much easier to produce when I have been working with a player or team for a good length of time, getting to know what really makes them tick as they labour to succeed.

Prior to the 2003 Rugby World Cup in Australia, it was easy to create some really powerful affirmations for the team, as the majority of them had been together as a unit for the past four years of training camps, Test matches and tours abroad. I also spent a great deal of time seeing players individually or in small groups with their club sides. Being so familiar with the work they'd put in and having got to know many of them personally, I was able to put together affirmations that emphasized what needed to be at the forefront of their minds if they were to achieve their potential on the field. I'd usually put them together and give them to the player the day before a match, so I could include anything specific to the opposition.

When putting together these affirmations, the principles are similar to the more general ones – written in the present tense and using powerful, emotive and, hopefully, inspirational language – but tailored for the specific situation. It is vital that there is an element of 'if I do this, I will get that'. The following affirmation was for one of the backs, who had a great deal of responsibility for managing the game and was also the goal kicker, prior to the biggest game of his life: the World Cup final.

- *I have worked harder and with greater intensity than most, and it is my intensity in practice that allows me to deserve success.*
- *My mind must be bigger than my body, so I am continually aware of all that is around me, to make effective decisions in the heat of battle.*
- *When I go for the posts, I will see every detail, the line, the smallest target and the piece of stitching, then drive the line with all my being.*
- *I have worked so hard for this, it is mine by right; I have earned it, I will relish the challenge and just love the occasion – this is my day.*

In the following affirmation, written for a back-row player whose job was to disrupt the opposition with his power and aggression, the player and I agreed that a vivid description of what to do and how that would feel, both physically and emotionally, would give him the best chance of performing well:

- *My enthusiasm for my continual improvement is the bedrock of my being.*
- *I play my best when I can flow with the game. My challenge is to find the flow on my own terms.*
- *I have my eyes wide open then beam on my target.*
- *I feel the turf and explosive energy under my feet.*
- *I will create the cocktail of hate, aggression, evil and dynamic power.*
- *I have soft hands and a decisive step.*
- *I will become nasty but be controlled and target my aggression.*

As with the previous pre-game affirmation, I set the scene with some powerful language, but I also included some process conditions – in other words, 'I will have a great performance *if I do X, Y and Z.'*

With golfers we'd have a routine. After they'd done their physical warm-up, we'd head to the driving range where, depending on the player, they would hit different shots, going through their clubs to achieve distances. We would then go to the short-game area for chips and bunker shots and then to the putting green, which is usually a short walk from the first tee. At this point I would pass them their written affirmation, which would hopefully capture the moment and inspire the player to perform at their best when it really mattered. Sometimes it's based on history, sometimes the previous round or tournament, or something they've been specifically working on. I try to inspire a bit of a fire-up, a bit of 'Wow!' and a reminder of the process and their proven ability.

At the start of Chapter 1, we saw a snippet from Luke Donald's affirmation at the Dubai World Championship and here is one for another golfer, prior to the last round of a tournament:

- *What a great opportunity to consolidate a deliberate pre-shot routine and test your resolve to:*
  - *maintain command posture with a tall neck*
  - *keep a mindset of arrogant expectation and perform through all levels of interference.*
- *Your vivid pre-shot routine creates a mental momentum and strength.*
- *Your command posture displaces any fatigue.*
- *Your arrogant expectation allows you to perform to your potential.*
- *Health warning: this only works if you have worked hard at all the components of your game – you have worked fucking hard!!!*

The aim of this was to make clear the importance of his posture – the process – and inspire a sense of inevitability about a great performance – an arrogant sense of destiny. I wanted him to be very aware of all the high-quality, hard work he'd put in and, as so much of that was around his pre-shot routine, I wanted him to recognize and derive confidence from this – which would feed into the rest of his game.

Your Own Affirmations

These affirmations aren't only the preserve of sports stars – we can all write our own and enjoy similarly powerful results, if we do them right. To ensure that your affirmations are effective, several protocols must be followed. They should be personal, written in the present tense and proactive. All the statements should be phrased positively – what you *want* to do rather than what you want to avoid – in strong, vivid, productive language. No wishy-washy hollow positives, please. While there is no 'I' in team, your affirmations should be packed full of them: all statements should be in the first person. They're about you as an individual: your performance; your actions; your feelings. And they should *only* be about yourself. The only person you are competing with is yourself – your previous performance levels and attitude.

Your affirmations should include accurate and realistically achievable goals that you are working towards. You should talk about accomplishments and goals in the present tense – right now – rather than sometime in the future. The language should be such that, like advertising slogans, it conjures up strong images, feelings and emotions: love, joy, pride, excitement, success – descriptive, action words.

If you were writing a trailer for a Hollywood action film, what kind of language would you use to try to attract an audience? Words such as 'exciting', 'thrilling' and 'daring' spring to mind, and it is this kind of language that belongs in your own affirmations to bring them to life. However, there is a caveat to all this:

your affirmations must be realistic and grounded in fact. You are not going to be on the verge of victory every time you perform, so the challenge must be relevant and realistic to you. While I have written affirmations for men about to play in a World Cup final or for a golfer about to play a round that could make him world number one, I've also written them for those looking to improve their score or hone a particular skill in an environment more relevant to them. Your event-specific affirmations could be before you deliver an important speech, before an interview or even before a particularly tough day at work, and your more general ones could be about improving your performance in meetings or asserting yourself at work – asking for a pay rise more frequently or making sure you leave on time more regularly. The point is that the goals should be realistic and identify processes that will improve your performance.

Also, grounding them in fact means that everything you put into your affirmation must be true. There'd be no point saying 'I've practised hard with great commitment' if it isn't true, any more than it would be for any of the people I've mentioned previously. It would be like building a castle on quicksand. If something isn't true then it has no place in an affirmation: we can convince ourselves of many things, but not if we know them to be categorically false.

I have listed some short statements below and given examples of how to bring them alive through powerful language:

Statement	Affirmation
I really work hard when I practise.	I work with a burning desire and intensity to continually improve.
I concentrate on my posture.	I work on creating a magnificent command posture; the greater the occasion, the bigger I am.

Statement	Affirmation
I try to look for the detail when I . . .	When I see the detail, my process is magnificently strong and I am wonderfully resilient.
I try to keep control when I play.	When I set my command posture I take control of the toughest situations.
I hope I can cope with this important event – I have practised hard.	I have prepared harder than I could have thought possible; I am excited and so ready for this.
Visualize.	I see every vivid detail.
I am ready.	I have power in abundance; my posture gives me absolute control.

These are just examples of how I would approach a general affirmation and I would obviously tailor the language for whoever I was coaching. When doing your own, either for yourself or for someone you are managing or coaching, it is up to you to choose the right language to get the best results. I understand that it can be a bit difficult to grasp at first, and that using this powerful, productive language might make you feel a bit embarrassed or as though you're treading in 'American self-help' territory. Remember, no one else – aside from yourself and either your manager or someone you're managing – is going to read it, so any self-consciousness about using language that might make you uncomfortable if it were read to a room should be put to one side. This is a very personal thing and should be treated as such. You are writing something to yourself, to fill your mind with images and feelings that will help you perform at the next level to where you are now.

Even the process of writing affirmations is beneficial in itself.

There is real value in spending the time to sit down, think about and then write down what it is that you want to achieve, in a 'how to' format and with powerful, motivational language.

I have constructed a few basic guidelines for your own affirmations, which could be adapted for sport, business – or anything you want:

- *List your qualities as a person, e.g. determined, hard working, skilful. They can even be what you would wish to be, such as, 'When I am determined I can achieve promotion.' So this becomes, 'When I do this [become determined], I will get that [promotion].'*
- *Try to get a clear view of the process or processes that will help you to perform, for example: 'When I take time to set my posture and rehearse the takeaway, my swing is much more consistent.'*
- *Always aim for improvement at your own margin. If you can run five kilometres and want to get to ten, work on achieving six first then gradually increase at your own margin: 'When I focus on counting the number of breaths I take, my rhythm and flow improves and I run with less effort; my challenge is to start the counting at four kilometres and let my body take over.'*
- *Try to work out the set process that gives you the platform to perform. This could be posture, talking to the back of the room, systematically making eye contact with someone: 'When I start the meeting, if I stand up straight and drop my shoulders down, then look at the person at the back of the room, I feel in command; my challenge is to do this every time. When I am in "command" I am at my most effective.'*

Outside my coaching in the sporting world, I have been working with a salesman in a German sports car dealership. He is not very confident in creating rapport with new customers and is always anxious about completing a sale – the point at which his job is at its most pressured. He becomes hurried, as he's so keen to make the sale that he forgets parts of the process and jumps to the outcome. Here is an affirmation we put together:

- *I am a smart, conscientious, well-trained sales person, naturally polite and courteous.*
- *When I take the time to find out specifics about my customer and take a genuine interest in their employment, family and interests, rather than concern myself with the sale straight away, I am more successful.*
- *My biggest challenge is to control my anxiety about making the sale. If I concentrate on my posture and adopt a relaxed demeanour, I will create a more relaxed environment for both me and my customer to operate in.*
- *When I take time, concentrate on the detail and continually follow the process, I will be successful.*

The most important point for the salesman to emphasize to himself is his need to stop and reset before going calmly through the steps to secure a sale. In this affirmation is another tip that you could take into your own. Here, we've taken his negative thoughts (about his anxiety at making a sale) and changed them into a more positive light – a glass is half-full approach – but equally there is a 'how to' attached to it and a sense of inevitability: 'If I do this, I will get that.' You could do the same with your own negative or self-doubting thoughts, reframing the language and adding a powerful 'how to'.

In most working environments there is a system of appraisals. Some of those working for particularly good companies might find themselves with a list of goals that they constantly have to work towards, providing regular feedback to their managers who review their progress as they go. Those are the lucky ones.

Many others simply agree to their goals, sign them off and then forget about them until the next appraisal a year down the line. Wouldn't it be a better idea to agree to a set of self-improving and skill-developing goals, producing affirmations together to go with them that you could keep to hand and refer to at the start of each day, updating them as you go along? They would, of course, need to adhere to my protocols of being achievable (at your margin – just one more . . .), building on existing work and ability, emotional (how you will feel) and, vitally, couched in powerful, productive language. Rather than having a set of woolly, indeterminate goals sitting in an unopened folder in a filing cabinet, wouldn't it be better to have a series of empowering statements to help you build towards these targets and make them feel a bit more visceral and real?

Better than Before: The No Limits Mindset

Friday, 19 March 2010: the day before England played France. Jonny Wilkinson hadn't made the team and would be on the bench for the Test and we were working together on the training ground at the Pennyhill Park Hotel, near Bagshot, Surrey. Because of the severe knee injury he had suffered, we had remodelled his kicking technique to avoid any hyperextension (when the leg extends beyond being straight). Out there in the cold, with him practising his technique despite not making the team, he gave it his all. Having been involved in over 160 international rugby Test matches and witnessed the 'Why bother, I'm on the bench?' mentality, I know for a fact that a lesser player would not have been so committed.

We tackled the last session as if he was just starting, not an ounce of effort lacking, and we went through the narrow-angle goal kicking, in which he would take kicks at goal from just inside the touchline and about five yards from the try line: a kick of about thirty yards at a target about a yard wide, at best. He took eight kicks – four from the left, four from the right – and made seven out of eight – with the one that missed hitting the post. It was a sensational display.

Jonny came off the bench with less than twenty minutes to go in the match, with England down by five points. Within five minutes they were awarded a penalty around the halfway line, near the touchline – a kick of well over fifty-five yards. Jonny nailed it and for the rest of the game France closed their play down to run down the clock and hang on for the final whistle – always fearful of another Wilkinson penalty.

Fast forward a year to 2011, when we were working together at Twickenham on the 'day off' in the lead-up to one of the Six Nations games. After a particularly taxing practice, in which his technique was fully put to the test, he proceeded to kick ten drop goals in a row, from over forty-five yards out, off my passing. Remarkable enough in itself, but he'd kicked them from alternate feet – left foot, right foot, left foot – and made all ten. *Better than before*, I thought to myself. *He really is a lot better than before.*

'Better than before' became our adopted mantra after his injury and I firmly believe that the Jonny Wilkinson of 2011 was better than the 2003 model. I'd even go so far as to say that the Jonny Wilkinson of 2014 was better still, a more complete kicker and player, not to mention captain of double Heineken Cup winners and Top 14 champions Toulon.

Injury is a very real risk for players across all sports and serious injury is particularly prevalent in the likes of football and rugby, where physical contact is permissible. So many players who suffer a severe injury – knee surgery, a broken leg, the list goes on – talk about getting back to the position they were in prior to the injury. 'Back to before' is their mantra. But I feel this is far too limiting, with getting 'back to before' setting that standard as your ceiling for improvement, and indeed it can become an almost illusory status, this 'before', that many can feel they'll never really achieve.

As time moves on we all develop, and for an elite sportsman or woman that should mean a continual commitment to improvement, just as it should for anyone in anything they do. Our maturity and our understanding of what we do should always be growing, and being injured is no excuse for stagnation. That is

not to underestimate exactly what a performer has to do to come
back from an injury: there are long, lonely hours in the gym,
with physiotherapists and doctors, away from the buzz and
camaraderie of teammates, the adulation of supporters and the
sheer, irreplaceable thrill of playing a sport you love and excel at.
A top-level career in sport is often not a long one and substantial
time out because of injury can significantly eat into this and certainly play on an athlete's mind.

But, as hard as it is, this time out should be used to continue a
player's development. If they can't play, they can still look at
their game and what they can do to improve it. If they can't exercise on an injured leg, perhaps they could use the time to
develop strength and fitness in other muscle groups. The experience of injury and being away from the game can help them
grow as people. And, on the road to recovery, if they're physically unable to do exactly what they could before, then they can
look at adapting to this, at acquiring new skills to compensate
and to progress, with the idea that you can come back *better than
before*.

Of course, it's very sad to watch some players return from
injury with their capacities clearly reduced. You tend to see it
most in players with great pace whose injuries slow them down
and they're unable to find ways to compensate. The former
England and Liverpool footballer Michael Owen springs to
mind – his pace helped scorch the image of his World Cup
1998 goal against Argentina into the international sporting consciousness, but as injuries reduced his pace and became so
recurrent, it sadly became the symbol of his career rather than
the beginning of it. With Jonny, it was a case of adapting his
technique so that he didn't hyperextend his leg and, allied to
his incredible work ethic and desire, he was able to come back
better than before.

Here is an affirmation for another international rugby player,
who had broken his wrist and was faced with a considerable time
out of the game:

- *I am a brave, fast, smart, tenacious player with a great feel for the game, and the ability to execute skills at real pace.*
- *I know now that I am only scratching the surface of my potential. I have become more systematic with my approach and attention to detail. I have now opened another world of potential.*
- *I am using my injury break to ensure that I return a better player than before, both physically and mentally, dramatically improving my speed of pass and becoming one of the few two-footed box kickers in the game.*
- *I cannot wait to play at a whole new exciting level. I am going to be a better player than I was before.*
- *I know now there really are no limits to the margins of my performance.*

This player was determined to take advantage of the break to work on areas that he otherwise would not have had the time to if he was playing. Together, we emphasized the desire to return better than before, which is also cloaked in the phrase 'I am only scratching the surface of my potential'.

We all have setbacks in our own lives and it's important to take a similar approach to them. The nearest comparison to a long break through injury I can think of is probably enforced unemployment, for example if you've been made redundant through work. This kind of break is obviously filled with financial worries that a wealthy professional sports star wouldn't be affected by, but the similar feelings of being isolated from your erstwhile colleagues and the worry about getting back to where you were before are all there. It may be that you will need to adapt too, not to a new method of kicking but to different financial circumstances or even a new career path, so it's equally important to have the perspective that things can be better than before. Simply trying to get 'back to before' can be elusive and difficult to achieve, certainly in the current economic climate, and being aware of the need to adapt, to accept that things may need to be different from before, is important. Being unemployed can be a lonely and dispiriting period in anyone's life, and this mantra of 'better than before', like the glass is half full, can be an important one to adopt.

'Better than before' is, of course, part of the no-limits mindset that I feel is essential for anyone – a top-level athlete, a first-jobber keen to climb the ladder or even an old hand at coaching – to adopt if they want to improve their performance. The no-limits mindset says that, no matter who you are, whatever your standard, everyone is capable of improving from where they are right now. No limits is all about improving upon *yourself* – not anyone else – and being the best that you can allow yourself to be.

When performers are described as 'special' or 'naturally gifted' we take this for granted, without stopping to think about the hours they have spent learning and practising 'special' skills by continually improving at the margins of their own performance. Cristiano Ronaldo, arguably the greatest footballer in the world, may have all sorts of natural genetic gifts, but he has also continually improved by pushing himself to be the best. The stories of his hard work on the training ground – stories that seem to be consistent with almost every one of the very top players in any sport – back this up and I can state categorically that the best players I have coached, the likes of Jonny Wilkinson, have worked tirelessly at pushing their own margins. Even now, at his peak, do you really think Cristiano Ronaldo doesn't believe he can get better?

It's this attitude, this mindset, that I strive to embed in every person I coach, be it the German car salesman, a professional golfer, a sixteen-year-old student desperate to improve her posture or a manager at the end of his career who has been there and done it all. I still believe anyone, no matter who, can get better – that there really are no limits to personal progression. Of course, this mindset needs to be created with the right language, which embeds the idea that we can improve as long as we work as hard as possible to achieve it – a continual step up on our previous selves. Performing under pressure is a skill and, like any skill, it can be learned and improved.

Through this no limits mindset, informed by no-limits language, a commitment to continual improvement can be attained. When the going gets tough and the pressure is really on, it can help bring perspective, to look at things with the desire to still do your best. There is no question in my mind that, no matter how dire a situation may be – missing the cut in a professional tournament, losing a match, facing a setback in your career – the commitment, discipline and tenacity to arrest the downward slide and finish by scoring a 'consolation' goal, moving marginally up the leader board or putting in that extra effort at work, even when it seems futile, can create a mental momentum which keeps the 'better than before' belief about yourself alive.

Principle 2: Language

Skilful use of language directly increases self-esteem and develops confidence: the fundamental prerequisite of your ability to perform at full potential under pressure.

Careless, clumsy, thoughtless use of language can destroy confidence and result in low self-esteem, which interferes with your ability to perform under pressure.

3. MANAGING LEARNING

3.

The Ugly Truth

The scene is an old hall in Sheffield, where four men are practising a dance routine with very little success to the sound of Donna Summer's 'Hot Stuff' blaring out of the cassette player.

The 'choreographer' – a middle-aged man who looks more at home in the boardroom than on the dance floor – is becoming increasingly exasperated by the inability of the four dancers to finish the routine in a straight line with their arms aloft. He's explained what he wants – and thought he'd made it very clear.

'All I want to do is get you in a straight bloody line! What do I have to do?' he cries.

'Well, it's the Arsenal offside trap,' one of the dancers says.

'You what?'

'The Arsenal offside trap. Lomper here,' he explains as he motions to one of the other dancers, 'is Tony Adams, right? Any bugger looks like scoring, we all step forward and wave our arms around like a fairy.'

'Oh, well that's easy,' another dancer, Dave, says.

'OK,' the choreographer concedes, turning to the young lad manning the cassette player and inviting him to press play again.

'Hot Stuff' starts up again and, after a 'One, two, three, go!' the four step forward with military precision and raise their right arms together while shouting, 'Ref!'

The Arsenal offside trap.

The choreographer, shaking his head, concedes: 'Perfect . . . perfect.'

'Well, you should have said,' says Dave, pouting and turning away in mild disgust.

The Meaning of the Message

The scene is from *The Full Monty*, a film about unemployed workers trying their hands at being professional male strippers – a pressured environment not many of us would feel comfortable entering into.

The choreographer in this scene is guilty of making the same mistake as so many coaches, teachers and managers. He is starting from his own version of reality rather than using that of those he is coaching. As one of the dancers points out, if he'd spoken to them in terms they could understand from the start, they'd have got it much sooner. It's fair to say that the meaning of the message is in the response you get. If you don't get the correct response then change the message.

As a coach, it is my responsibility to manage people's learning so that they can perform at their best, and this invariably means learning to see things from their point of view so that I can use the tools that will best apply to them. During my PhD research, which involved working with elite kickers in rugby, I would give different messages – verbal keys – to each of the players, even though each message pertained to the same process: kicking from hand. Effectively I was reframing the process for each player. For one it would be 'On the shelf, through the gate', an instruction to hold the ball in both hands and imagine placing it on an imaginary shelf in front of their hips; once the ball had been 'placed' (i.e. released), the gate was the gap between the hands that now acted as a guide to swing the kicking leg through. Another player might prefer the prompt 'Right foot, left hand' to swing the (right) foot through the ball so it finished next to their left hand. There is no right and wrong; it's about developing a range of different keys, then finding out what works best for each player. I doubt very much that the Arsenal offside trap is standard dance choreography.

A friend of mine recently enrolled for golf lessons. When I asked him how it was going after three sessions, he gave a non-committal 'OK.' When pushed, he relented and told me he had learned about the grip, the stance and the swing plane. Impressive. But when I asked him how his game was, he sheepishly replied, 'I don't know – we're not allowed to hit balls yet.'

This is classic 'instruction', in which the theory – the comprehensive list of 'what to do' before you even play – is given too much weight right at the start, without any of the activity itself. How often have you been instructed on how to do something at work that doesn't really register until you start doing it yourself? The overriding philosophy behind the Pressure Principle's third strand – Managing Learning – is to start with where *you* are in *your* development. If you think about my friend and his golf lessons, how would the instructor even have known the level he was playing at, or where he needed most help? My friend eventually quit his lessons, saying it was too complicated and boring.

In 1993, a study led by Swedish psychologist Anders Ericsson derived the '10,000 hour rule', which maintains that 10,000 hours of deliberate practice are necessary to become an expert performer, be it in sport, the arts or science. The key word here is *deliberate*, but what might be more worrying to those about to embark on a 10,000-hour odyssey is the language used by psychologist Christian Jarrett to describe this practice: 'You don't just repeat what you know, but instead constantly seek to stretch yourself [which involves] forensic self-criticism, repeated failure and a dogged ability to keep dusting yourself down and trying again – a process that is not particularly enjoyable.' Sound appealing? If all this deliberate practice is going to be tough, demoralizing, frustrating and full of angst, then the likelihood of most people sticking with it and progressing is slim.

Does this mean we can't enjoy learning if we want to get to a standard above where we currently are – that we shouldn't get excited about the possibilities of what we can achieve? In the right environment, with effective language and emphasis on managing learning rather than instruction, developing new skills or improving existing ones can be immensely fun and satisfying – and this chapter will illustrate exactly why that is so important.

I'm not suggesting for a second that learning is easy – far from it. And, while it isn't necessarily possible to always find hours of demanding practice enjoyable, there should be some sense of progression and satisfaction, otherwise it's too easy to step away. Recognizing what you *can* do is the place to start and the philosophy that anyone can improve in any field they choose – it isn't the exclusive preserve of the elite performer – is the mindset to adopt. However, anyone looking to improve must be prepared to go to a place I call the ugly zone.

The Ugly Zone

'I messed up.'

'I can't play this piece properly.'

'I hit the ball in the water *again*!'

When you are attempting to master a new skill or improve on an existing one, and you're trying and failing to correct something you've done wrong, you're in the ugly zone.

The ugly zone is the place where your execution does not match your intention. The ugly zone doesn't discriminate among tasks – you could be learning a new dance routine, playing a piece of music or hitting a golf ball – and the ugly zone is no respecter of talent or ability: the very best find themselves in the ugly zone as well as complete novices. But the very best find their way out again with more success. The ugly zone is the place where you try and fail, try again and fail – and continue trying and failing. It's the area just beyond your present ability.

A cricketer practising with the bowling machine set at a relatively sedate 65 mph would have plenty of time to see the ball and play the shot with the middle of the bat. If the machine increased to 75 mph, it would require more concentration with the reduced time to play the shot, but a top player shouldn't miss often. Once the machine is cranked up to 85 mph, the player has lost the overriding sense of control they had before, and with so little time to prepare they edge or miss the ball quite frequently. Finally, the machine starts spewing out balls at 90 mph and the player is under siege, struggling to get any real control, failing to react effectively in time and playing and missing with alarming regularity. They're in their ugly zone.

If you're a keen runner, what would it take for you to get into your ugly zone? If you can run five kilometres in thirty minutes quite comfortably and you wanted to improve your time to under twenty-five minutes, you would need to commit to running the first half of the race in under twelve and a half minutes. This unfamiliar, more demanding pace would likely see you reach your ugly zone after halfway, with the last third particularly tough. It would demand more effort and determination and an ability to tolerate increasing levels of physical discomfort. You might feel a stitch coming on, or struggle to regulate your breathing. You might not make it under twenty-five minutes. You might give up.

The ugly zone can be a difficult place to be physically but, more importantly, it demands a great deal of mental energy – imagine the unhelpful thoughts the runner might experience, urging them to quit, or the mental energy required to do it again and again as they fail to reach their target. The ugly zone can be demoralizing in the extreme, but it is where true improvement can be achieved.

Many of us, if we're honest, often find it difficult to break out of our comfort zone. You might go for a run round the park reasonably regularly, but a lap is quite enough, thank you. Or, if you're musically inclined, you might have a tinkle on the ivories every so often, but you'll play something familiar that you can play well. And what about at work – do you spend much time outside your comfort zone there?

Our brains can be pretty lazy. They naturally want to conserve energy and are happy to coast along in familiar territory. In Figure 2 you can see that the comfort zone requires very little cognitive energy.

In the comfort zone, our brains continue to do what they are already familiar with and it's a very efficient state, energy wise, to be in, which is why it's so easy to coast along there. However, in the ugly zone, where learning something new happens, the brain expends a great deal of energy as you attempt to do something you cannot already do.

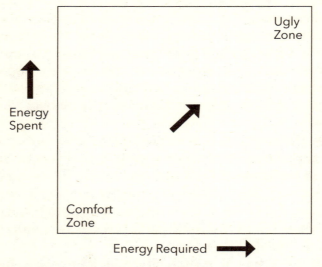

Figure 2 *The ugly zone*

Source: Adapted from the Energy Model developed by strategic neuroscientist Marie de Guzman, Newman Sumner Ltd.

When the brain learns something new, it creates new neural pathways which demand energy. Initially, these pathways are quite fragile, but with more practice they become stronger and more efficient. Imagine that your first attempt at learning a skill – hitting a cricket ball at 90 mph, learning a new piece of music, accessing a new system at work – is like hacking a path through a forest for the first time. Clearing the path would no doubt feel strange, awkward and difficult – and demand a great deal of energy. Subsequent journeys would be easier – but certainly not easy – and you'd probably have some setbacks on the way, but eventually you'll start to travel faster, with each repetition requiring slightly less energy.

In the end, what was once a jungle path has become a motorway, with lots of traffic (brain signals) moving very fast along it. You can now execute the skill in your comfort zone.

This is all the result of continual practice, making it easier to perform the skill each time you try it. To give you a rough idea of how long it can take to master, it is an accepted convention that it takes at least forty days to change a golf swing, with the time period extended for every day that the new swing isn't used.

The challenge most of us face is that our brains are essentially efficient organs – or lazy, depending on your point of view – and they want to stay in the comfort zone, where they can conserve energy. They don't want to spend forty consecutive days practising a golf swing. The brain is wary of committing to the ugly zone. So how do we make it go there?

The Childlike Approach

John is five years old and, like many a child whiling away the time over the school summer holidays, he's grown bored with kicking his football around outside now that the World Cup is over and he's watching the golf on television with his dad, fascinated by the adulation and excitement that hitting a small ball through the air with a club seems to generate.

John watches the golfer on television, who takes some swings at nothing with his club, before standing very still over the ball, slowly bringing his club back and then – *whoosh!* He hits the ball skyward, flying away, before landing near a flag and the crowd goes wild, cheering and shouting (or at least offering some very polite applause – this is golf, after all). *It's almost like scoring a goal!*

He watches every detail, taking in the player's little salute in acknowledgement of the crowd and his brisk march to his next shot. *Time for me to have a go*, thinks John.

Armed with a plastic club and a sponge ball from his toy box, John heads outside to tee off in his inaugural garden championship. He puts the ball down, settles himself like the player on television, takes aim and then – *nothing!* He missed, but thinks nothing of it and simply tries again. This time, he scuffs the ball, nudging it a couple of feet forward in the grass. Still no reaction. John swings again and this time the ball nestles a few yards ahead on top of the grass.

With the image of the television player firmly in his mind, John approaches the ball once again. He takes a swing and then – *whoosh!* The ball is airborne and floats far down the garden fairway. The applause is ringing in his ears as he takes off his imaginary hat, saluting the crowd. With the excitement and joy full to bursting within him, John cannot wait to take his next shot.

He fluffs it, sending the ball trundling through the grass, before he remembers that his success came when the ball was perched on top of the grass. He tries again and – *whoosh!* This time he raises a modest hand to the warm applause from the crowd.

Let's wind the clock forward twenty-four years. John is now nearly thirty and works in a bank. He did well at school, got a good degree at university and has kept up a keen interest in sport, playing cricket in the summer and football in the winter. Golf hasn't entirely disappeared from his life – he's a member of the local golf club, though, by his own admission, he is not a good golfer. 'I find it too frustrating,' he says. 'It's OK until I make a mistake, and then I fall apart.'

Today is his company's annual golf day. John is anxious to perform well, but he certainly doesn't see his anxiety as a positive thing. He watches his two playing partners tee off, both of them hitting shots that land in the middle of the fairway. John is up now.

Determined to hit the ball as hard as he possibly can, John swings with all his might – and the ball squirts through the grass and settles just past the ladies' tee. 'Damn, that happens every time I use this effing driver!' he thunders, jamming the club back into his bag and slouching over to take his next shot. He doesn't have to walk far before selecting a new club and, still fuming, he lashes his shot into the trees – taking a divot the size of a small garden with it.

'I might as well give up this pigging game,' he mutters as he begins his slow march towards the trees, his colleagues looking on in horror. But, to his surprise and only a slight degree of relief, he discovers that the ball has landed kindly, on a flat piece of grass in a clearing with the green in sight.

Convinced of his own capacity for disaster, John takes a seven iron and, stuck in a mental state somewhere between rage, surrender and suicide, he barely even takes aim – *what would be the point?* – before he swings and, to his total surprise, a wonderfully solid clink pierces the calm and his ball whistles through the air, fades away and lands softly, rolling to an enticing position of stillness a mere two and a half feet from the pin. His playing partners, no doubt having dreaded the thought of another seventeen holes of *that*, offer warm congratulations on a terrific shot. 'About time I did something right,' John mutters ungraciously.

Finally, John gets out his putter for the short putt to make par. Summoning a bit of the old Dunkirk spirit, he announces: 'These putts are a lot more difficult than they look.' He proceeds to push it wide and a couple of feet past the hole, following it up with a

verbal tirade as amusing as it is biologically impossible. His playing partners attempt to calm him down – it was a great approach
shot to the green and he's only one over par, after all – but it's all
in vain.

What has happened to John during those twenty-four years?
His entire approach to the game – a mindset of fun, enjoyment,
performance, expectation and learning – has been completely
reversed. His five-year-old self celebrated what he achieved. He
relived his good shots and was desperate to repeat them, while
the adult John's so-called 'childish' outbursts simply reinforced
the very behaviour he was so desperate to avoid.

The truth is that we can learn a good deal from our youthful
approach to challenges. A twenty-nine-year-old man can learn
much from a five-year-old in their ability to take on a task with
enthusiasm and excitement. Young children get into the ugly
zone very easily. They have an instinctive, relentless curiosity and
hunger to learn new things and they have none of the fear of failure that inhibits an adult. They love the thrill of learning, and
when it gets tough and they fail at it, well, they just try again . . .
and again – attempting to work out what they need to do differently. How much more easily than an adult is a child able to learn
to ride a bike, speak a new language or learn to swim?

One would hope that children receive nothing but encouragement from their parents as they try new things, so their self-
esteem is high, there is no negative consequence of failure and,
once they stop, they're often mentally exhausted and go to sleep
for an hour or so, before waking up and doing it all again with
the same enthusiasm and commitment. What a great mindset to
bring to learning to perform in a pressure environment!

Young children don't suffer many of the consequences of
pressure that an adult has to deal with. While we can never
go back to our childlike selves, surely we can take something
from our youthful approach to learning. We could slip straight
into the ugly zone as children and we must look to providing
the similar conditions of childhood to recreate this: continual

encouragement, rewarding and reinforcing success, keeping self-esteem and energy levels high. Children throw themselves into their ugly zone while they're practically drowning in excitement (to play) and have no fear of failure. While we've talked in Chapter 1 about turning our anxiety into a childlike excitement, our adult minds still present a testing challenge for us to get into the ugly zone.

Negative Bias

Learning is not limited to the challenge of creating neural pathways. The brain works in negatives and positives, like an internal balance sheet, and the problem for the learner is that the brain is negatively biased, so that negative influences and evaluations have a more powerful effect on the mind than positive information.

As Roy Baumeister, Francis Eppes Professor of Psychology at Florida State University, writes:

Perhaps the broadest manifestation of the greater power of bad events than good to elicit lasting reactions is contained in the psychology of trauma . . . Many kinds of traumas produce severe and lasting effects on behavior, but there is no corresponding concept of a positive event that can have similarly strong and lasting effects. In a sense, trauma has no true opposite concept.

Furthermore, the brain typically avoids situations that it perceives to have potentially negative outcomes. Baumeister goes on to say: 'A given increase in possible loss therefore has a bigger impact on a decision than an objectively equal increase in possible gain.'

Our minds can be risk-averse organs if left unchecked, and the potential mental and physical anguish that could lie in store for someone entering their ugly zone is a risk. Table 3 outlines some

Table 3 Leading our brains to the ugly zone

Negatives: Why we want to stay in our comfort zone	Positives: Why we should progress to our ugly zone
Self-esteem: anything that has a potential failure is a threat to self-worth	Make explicit all elements of success; the level of commitment is the most important element to commend
Anything that is not immediately successful has a high risk of perceived failure and energy spend	Be realistic about the length of time required to master the skill and highlight marginal improvements in the process
Social: I have to be seen by my peers to be successful; the ugly zone with angst and frustration is not for me	Commend effort and the commitment to get in the ugly zone. Angst and frustration are by-products of commitment and desire – well done!
Put off before they start by seeing the outcome so far away from the intended outcome	Take away the outcome, concentrate on building the parts of the process, celebrate progress based on previous self (no limits)
Use of language: allowing what you want to *avoid* to get into the brain	Always focus on what you *want* to do – productive language
Past use of universal statements: 'I *always* mess this up'	Take apart these statements: 'every time' usually does not mean every single time; highlight when it has worked or when you have improved
Fatigue: it is tough to stay in the ugly zone	Work little and often: twenty minutes' practice every day, rather than three hours once a week

of the negative thoughts that can prevent us making it to our ugly zone and how we might counter them.

The strongest negatives are fear of potential failure and looking foolish in front of your peers. It's rarely just a case of 'I can't be bothered' (although this clearly is a factor for some). People will always find reasons why they can't do something, or argue that they shouldn't be doing it anyway. You've probably seen a similar reaction to a new protocol or training opportunity at work. You might think that top sports professionals, on their never-ending odyssey of improvement, would be immune to this. You'd be wrong.

What Will Other People Think?

To become a top sports star requires huge levels of self-belief, much as it would to get to the top of any industry; the top people in business or government are driven as a necessity by huge amounts of confidence in themselves. But in sport there aren't many hiding places if that belief doesn't have some justification. The best in sport have risen through intense amounts of competition in the school and youth levels and fought their way through the professional ranks to take their seats at the top table. While the very best usually have no problem at all with the idea that they're continually improving (Cristiano Ronaldo; Jonny Wilkinson) there are some for whom, after rising to their position in the game, getting in the ugly zone – trying and failing, or, worse, *being seen* trying and failing – can be a real pinprick to their self-image and damaging to their confidence, the lifeblood of any elite performer. Self-esteem and self-worth can potentially be damaged by 'failure' and this can be a serious impediment to getting in the ugly zone.

To be seen to be failing in front of one's peers is difficult in any walk of life. Pressure of this sort can be stressful and hard to manage, as no one wants to be seen to be holding a group back, or the one who can't master a skill. We all learn different things at different speeds, and only through commitment to the process can we hope to safely navigate the ugly zone and master a task. But some people will go to great lengths not to have to subject themselves to the spectacle of failure and it's an attitude that can be contagious.

I did some work at Watford Football Club for Aidy Boothroyd, their manager, in the 2006–07 season, when they had been promoted to the Premier League. Aidy was an extremely committed manager and they had a good squad, with the likes of Manchester United's promising young goalkeeper Ben Foster on loan and the forward Ashley Young, who would transfer to Aston Villa later that season. My job was to work with small groups within the squad to improve their kicking, with the emphasis on getting the players to move from a C-shape kick to a J-shape (see Chapter 1).

Ben Foster had phenomenal power and we worked on tempering this and improving his control. With the defenders and midfielders we worked on hitting passes that could quickly turn defence into attack – with counterattacking a vital tactic for any newly promoted team likely to be battling relegation. These players were all a joy to work with. They found some of the practices demanding, but they stuck to them and started showing some real improvement. They were a real tribute to Aidy's culture of continual improvement.

Then it came to working with the forwards. They certainly didn't lack for skill, but their attitude was a different matter. I worked with them on their running half-volleys when shooting at goal, with a target in the netting for them to hit. Like the other players before them, they struggled a bit with this, particularly with their posture and timing. I encouraged them as I'd done before, explaining that, while it was difficult, it would make a big difference to their shooting in the long run. The players seemed to buy into it, except for one striker.

He really struggled with the task and his timing, so he started deflecting this by joking and messing around. It was as though he felt it was OK for him to give up because it demanded effort. What was of even more concern was the impact his behaviour had on the other players. They too pulled back from giving their all and the session ended, to my mind at least, a shambles.

In the next session I showed the forwards a video of Cristiano Ronaldo executing the skill I was attempting to get them to master, asking them to pay particular attention to his posture as he struck the ball. A few of the players sheepishly agreed and admitted that, when they got their body position right, the ball really flew. Sadly, once on the training field the session deteriorated as before, with the same player ducking out of the challenge of mastering the running half-volley. When I had a word, he told me he was only taking part because the manager had told him to. I responded that his influence was detrimental to the group and he was affecting the others. Another mistake, as he seemed to relish his influential status.

It's a cliché in sport to say that you'd never wish injury on another professional and it's a cliché I happen to subscribe to. But I can't pretend that fortune wasn't smiling kindly on me when the disruptive player was injured the following weekend and put out of action for a while. The next session was fantastic, with the players beginning to enjoy and benefit from the work we were doing. Ashley Young really developed his shooting and crossing, and it came as no surprise to see him eventually play for Manchester United.

I hadn't appreciated until then just how deep the influence of peer-group pressure can be, and it showed how important the attitude of influential people in any organization can be in shaping working culture for better or worse. I can't help but think how different the England Rugby World Cup squad of 2003 were, where the senior pros, led by Martin Johnson, supported the culture Clive Woodward implemented.

In the average yoga class it is not uncommon to see people in their sixties practising alongside those in their twenties, and a gravity-defying yogi alongside a stiff-as-a-board beginner – all with the common aim of improving themselves. In this kind of environment people seem eager to get into their ugly zones – stretching further, adopting ever-deeper poses – and work at their own pace and bodily limitations without fear of recrimination.

We need to foster similar environments at work, at home and in our sporting pursuits, where it is OK to improve upon ourselves and only ourselves, to work hard and within our own limitations. A place for learning where success is in achievable margins, so that it's just around the corner, not miles away, and where there is no negativity to be seen in failing at something in the quest for improvement – where it's OK to get ugly and try and fail and try again . . .

But there's something else we need to be clear about too: success and improvement won't happen overnight.

No Quick Fixes

We live in 'instant' times. We only have to reach into our pockets for our smartphones to find out the answer to a question. With music we flick through the tracks, give it a minute and move on. And this means that *investment*, of both time and effort, can be lacking when it comes to improving ourselves.

Without 'instant' results, many of us are inclined to give up. We try once, maybe twice, and if we're not successful we've had enough. Perseverance is a difficult concept for some of us, but if you look at a child learning, they simply don't understand the word 'can't': they'll play until they've tired themselves out.

If we're not successful straight away, our internal balance sheet, giving extra weight to the negatives, comes into play: *I can't do this right now; I don't want to be a failure; this could take up a lot of energy.* Before we're even conscious of it, we've given up.

This lack of immediate results is perhaps the biggest obstacle of all. How many times have you started at the gym or an exercise class, gone a couple of times and, in the absence of instant improvement, stopped, leaving costly memberships unused? It's likely you're not even aware that you've quit: 'I'll start properly next week/month, when I have more time . . .' But make no mistake, that is what has happened – and continuing to pay won't change it.

Simply signing up or starting to do something almost always isn't enough. It's necessary to make a full *investment*, so that the first time there is an obstacle you don't walk away. Getting in the ugly zone requires a commitment: going to the gym a couple of times isn't going to show results – it's madness to expect it to. Going at least three times a week over a period of months and gradually pushing at your margins – that will certainly improve your fitness. A couple of piano lessons aren't going to make you a pianist: weeks of lessons and practice gradually will.

When coaching, managing or teaching anyone making such a commitment, it is vital continually to reinforce their successful progress. I might say, 'Most people would have given up an hour ago, but you're better than that,' to someone in their ugly zone to keep up their motivation. And it's important to point out the bits that someone is doing correctly, to give some positives to that internal balance sheet.

Such continual motivation is essential to keep yourself going into the ugly zone. If, like the running example we mentioned earlier, you're training by yourself and trying to improve your time, you need to deliver these in a self-talk, so that you can look at what you've achieved. That will reinforce the balance sheet and show it's worth persevering. Even if you're making slow progress you might say: 'I'm achieving success – I'm a few seconds faster than I was last week and I'm not as sore the day after. If I keep going I can chip away at that time.'

Of course, many people choose to join clubs to have that encouragement come from others – when peer pressure can be positive. Personal trainers are another useful resource. It's much easier to quit on yourself than it is when you have someone you're paying by the hour pushing you and encouraging you when you're getting ugly.

From a coach's perspective, it's also important to get the 'how to' for the next step in there too. For example, when teaching someone to putt in golf it's very common for the body to sway with the stroke, which compromises control of the putter. The first step is to make the learner aware of what they are doing and then address it by, say, balancing a club against their backside – anything to make them conscious of holding their body still from the waist down and only moving their arms and shoulders. Of course, it's a natural reaction at having to keep one part of the body still to stiffen up altogether, which can leave them losing the 'feel' of rolling the putt. Usually, that makes them hit the ball too hard, well past the hole – and produces even worse results than their initial, body-swaying attempts.

The obvious response is, 'You hit it too hard – try to hit more softly,' but stating the obvious can be unhelpful when someone getting ugly is thinking: 'I did what you told me and my shot went twenty feet past the hole!' Better to say something like: 'Don't worry about that – your stability was perfect from the waist down. Well done. Now, see if you can keep your bottom half stable as before, but keep your shoulders loose so you can control the ball. This will take time, but you've nailed the hardest part already.'

Say to yourself: *I have been successful* [brain, take note] *and I know it's going to take some time* [I have been told so]. *If I have already been successful, it's worth me carrying on as the mental energy spent has created a higher chance of future success.*

Any organization, whether a running club or a business, should instil a culture of 'busy getting better', in which people can be constantly improving at the margins of their own performance. It's down to you to respond.

When I started working with fly-half George Ford at Leicester back in 2010, he wasn't getting much game time. For a young man itching to play, watching from the sidelines can be frustrating and, quite naturally, he was finding it tough to keep practising and get ugly, particularly on his weaker left foot. We would talk about his progress and about how at that age he had his whole career in front of him, and that time spent not playing should be seen as an opportunity to get 'busy getting better' for when the call came. George showed a maturity beyond his years with his outstanding mindset, always willing to get ugly during this period even though the short-term benefits weren't clear. After moving to Bath in 2013, he broke into the England squad the following season, four years after we had started working together.

A good approach to encourage people (or yourself) into the ugly zone is to identify and commend what has been done well, no matter the outcome. Break the task down into parts, with step-by-step outcomes to target (like reaching certain points of a piece of music, breaking each thirty-second barrier when running, keeping the bottom half of your body still when putting), and use productive language. Most important is that working in the ugly zone should be done 'little and often'.

Little and Often

Learning requires both mental and physical energy – consistently being in the ugly zone is demanding and tiring. To beat the fatigue, the most effective approach to learning any skill is to do it little and often rather than keeping on until you get it right.

Energy is a limited resource, so it is better to learn only when you are fresh. One familiar argument is that you'll have to perform when you're tired and under pressure, so you should train in the same circumstances. I agree that it is useful to practise acquired skills under these conditions, but pressure isn't helpful when you're learning the skills for the first time.

Regular progress on a daily basis – still challenging, but

harnessing all your energy each time to make an efficient effort – will produce far better results than compressing a month's worth of practice into a week, with your energy diminishing and the work you do becoming less and less effective. You might begin the next day still fatigued – or you might be so fed up you just want to quit.

Our brains will make the new neurological pathways in the ugly zone as long as there is the requisite mental commitment and energy, even working on them during our sleep, but when the energy depletes, so does the efficiency of our improvement. The mind is looking for the more heavily weighted negatives, and overdoing it without the corresponding level of improvement is yet another black mark in the internal balance sheet. Think about it: if you were revising for a test next week, which approach would you imagine to be more effective – an hour's revision each day or five hours' cramming the night before? As psychologist Professor John Dunlosky writes:

> *Although cramming is better than not studying at all in the short term, given the same amount of time for study, would students be better off spreading out their study of content? The answer to this question is a resounding 'yes'.*

When I am working with rugby kickers, I like to have indoor facilities, particularly when getting a player to learn or develop a new skill. I am regularly greeted with the riposte: 'But they kick in the wind!'

Yes, they do, but the players should learn the skill in an environment where the flight of the ball is a direct consequence of their kick, without any external factors. Get the learning done and then practise in the wind once the basics have been mastered. In reality, it would be ideal to have indoor sessions to refine and establish technique, coupled with regular practice outdoors. The bedrock of the progress of Stuart Barnes and Jonathan Webb – England rugby players with whom I worked at the start of the nineties – was regular early morning sessions at Bristol Grammar School's indoor cricket nets in their sports hall. A crucial part of Jonny Wilkinson's practice during his time at Newcastle Falcons involved using the indoor facilities at both Middlesbrough and Newcastle United football clubs. To give you an idea of just how highly we valued these sessions, it took up to an hour and a half to drive to Middlesbrough's indoor training facility from the Falcons' training ground.

Little and often should be your mantra so that you can immerse yourself in the ugly zone repeatedly. During the 2003 Rugby World Cup campaign with England, the backs would do a ten- to fifteen-minute kicking and catching practice at the end of each training session, which could be twice a day. These short, sharp and intense bouts of practice, in which the players would be pushed to the margins of their ability, are the kind of blueprint you could take into your own life. Many people have extremely busy work and family lives, but if you could fit in just half an hour at the end of your working day, every day, be it to practise on the piano or work on that 5k run, then, provided it is an intense session, you can reap the benefits from even a small amount of regular time in the ugly zone.

Another rationale for little and often is the process of physically and mentally resetting for the task at hand. Take free shots in basketball. Your first few attempts are likely to be all over the place as you find your range and home in on the correct trajectory. You might hit the backboard; you might drop short: each shot gives you more information to fine tune the next attempt. After a while, you will become more consistent, but if you were playing in a match, how many attempts would you get? So the key is to be successful first time, without any practice. If you put pauses into your practice, where you take a break and reset, you'll experience the feeling of that first shot more often. This is also why the pre-shot routine is so important to many skills that are executed under pressure: you only get one shot at it.

Eureka!

When we're working in the ugly zone, often after a lot of angst and frustration and trying and failing, we suddenly have a 'eureka' moment: the basketball shot sails perfectly through the hoop; we play a tricky bit of the piece we're learning beautifully on the piano; our putt drops with a satisfying 'plop!' into the hole. We've done it! And then we try to repeat our success and we fail. What's gone wrong? We can do this, can't we?

This happens when, instead of resetting our minds, getting back to the mental state in which we approached the first successful attempt, we get excited and rush straight into it again, taking it for granted that we'll succeed . . . and suddenly we're back in the ugly zone.

I've also seen rugby goal kickers and golfers who, after working in the ugly zone on their posture and sequencing, were able to kick the ball or strike it from the tee with great distance and little conscious effort. But then they think: 'If I'm hitting it this well with this amount of effort, what can I do if I really smash it?' This is what I call 'letting your horns grow'. The rugby player then starts to send his kicks astray, the golfer watches his balls sail off course into the rough. All the work that they have done is compromised by this desire to really smash it, causing an energy leak in their overreaching, inefficient sequence. The controlled focus on the process has gone out the window.

Resetting our minds, much like our posture, is therefore essential to get these consistent results – and, while our first success should certainly be acknowledged and celebrated, it's vital not to get too carried away by it. There's still a way to go before mastery is achieved.

I am all too aware of how easy and natural it is to want to stay in the comfort zone. It simply isn't possible to master something new without getting ugly, but I want to go back to the child's attitude to learning I touched upon earlier. If you can rekindle that youthful enthusiasm for knowledge and overcome the brain's natural resistance, then it is possible to create a sense of excitement about adding a new string to your bow, in much the same way that it is possible to turn your feelings of anxiety into excitement. Little and often means that you won't view your learning as an insurmountable challenge. You won't sit at the piano for hours on end trying to get it right and then quit when you can't. You'll do little chunks, note by note, pushing yourself each time and eventually putting it all together into a perfect whole. You'll have regular feedback and the continual improvement will boost your self-esteem. Instead of waiting a week between mammoth sessions, giving you time to dwell on what might or did go wrong, the little-and-often approach lets you focus on the building blocks of the task, gradually assembling them day by day without becoming intimidated by the looming objective on the horizon.

Outcome Avoidance

When learning a new skill, particularly one where the final outcome is clear to see, there is often a conflict between working on the small process you're getting ugly with and the overall big picture. If you're learning a piece of music, it's easier to break it into sections and work on each one without worrying too much about the final outcome (playing the piece as a whole); however, if you're working on your golf shot off the tee and you're addressing a specific area of your stroke or posture, it's impossible to avoid seeing the outcome (where the ball goes) and difficult not to be distracted; the brain is trying to avoid the negative – the bad shot. When working on a new aspect in a process, it's common for the outcome to suffer in the short term. But when you watch your shot slice far off course, it's difficult not to become more concerned about this than the adjustment you're making to your swing.

I commonly experience this in my work with rugby kickers. It's a real advantage in the game to be able to kick with both feet, so I often work with kickers on their weaker foot. When I start coaching a player I will always ask them to take the kick bearing in mind the technical advice I have to offer – and be clear that I don't care where it goes. But it doesn't matter what I say; if the eyes see it, the brain registers it – and it's impossible to remove this from a player's mind.

So I like to remove the outcome from their sight altogether. It's a practice I used years ago with Stuart Barnes and Jonathan Webb, when I'd get them to practise kicking balls into soccer nets in the park the morning before a game; these days I have players kick into special nets about three yards in front of them. This takes away the outcome and ensures all thoughts are on the process – the only feedback the players have is sound and feel. With Stuart and Jonathan, experienced players who knew what a good kick felt like, the last thing we wanted to do was get their critical brain in gear with thoughts about outcome on the morning of a game – they just needed to feel confident and ready to play.

The player learning to kick with their weaker foot will make quicker progress if they start with the kicking net. They will be able to focus on adopting the correct posture – right-footed players often naturally take up a right-footed posture even when kicking with their left, which is something that needs adjusting – and getting other processes right before worrying about bisecting the posts with their kicks.

Of course, it's not just for the weaker foot that removing the outcome can be a useful tool. When players are low on confidence or need to work on a specific part of their kick, it's useful to use the net. Players low on confidence have often become completely focused on their (negative) outcome and are no longer fully committing to their process. When the pressure is on and there is anxiety about the outcome (the ball going between the posts), it often becomes difficult to commit to the process (kicking *through* the ball). Introducing the net and removing the outcome allows them to recapture that solid thump on impact that marks a sweet strike and re-establish the trust in their process.

I remember a particular session with Jonny Wilkinson on the Twickenham turf of a Test week. He wasn't happy with his strike and was struggling to feel an inevitability about the outcome; my concern was that he'd allowed his thoughts about the out-come to distract him from the process. I lined up the ball for him to go for a forty-five-yard kick and then brought out the kicking net and put it three yards in front of the tee. After a few kicks the sound of the contact changed to a satisfying deep thud and occa-sionally he smashed the net at the top of the frame and toppled the whole thing over – which takes some doing.

Using the net, he was totally committed to kicking through the ball and absorbing the little adjustments in posture I sug-gested, so that when I took away the net, looked him in his good eye (the other was black from the previous game) and said, 'I don't care where this ball goes but I want you to commit to kick-ing through the ball,' he fired it straight through the posts – and well beyond them. His total commitment to the process ensured that the outcome – as well as his ear-to-ear grin afterwards – took care of itself.

Practice nets at cricket clubs and golf courses are perfect for this kind of outcome-avoiding practice. Stay clear of the driving range, where the outcome will be all too clear, and use these nets where the only feedback will be the feel of the shot. Golf is an extremely mentally demanding sport, especially for the part-time amateur. There is a tendency to start steering shots and manipu-lating your swing as soon as a couple of shots go astray, and working in the nets can allow you to focus entirely on your process – without watching another shot head dispiritingly for the rough.

Children are often helped to avoid an unwelcome outcome. While learning to swim, armbands and flotation aids are widely used to avoid sinking, while stabilizers prevent those learning to ride a bicycle from crashing straight to earth. Such aids allow us to practise the necessary individual components of an activity, so that when the armbands are deflated and the stabilizers unbolted, we are better equipped to deal with the outcome, whether that's a smooth swim across the pool and a seamless glide along the street, or sinking like a stone and wiping out by the kerb.

It sounds counterintuitive not to worry about the result of your action. But on a piano you wouldn't attempt to play a whole piece of music through, demoralizing yourself in the process, if you weren't ready, just as you wouldn't attempt to master a new piece of computer software in one go at work. And when working on a golf swing, or learning to swim or to ride a bicycle, or anything where the outcome is right in front of you, it's important to find ways to mask the outcome from your mind. It should be all about the process.

Matching Intentions

Golf day. Your ball has landed 130 yards from the green. The pin is four yards from the left side, guarded by a bunker next to a large tree. You have decided to aim a couple of yards right of the pin. You visualize your shot, see it landing on the green next to the flag. You set yourself, bring back the club and swing fluidly – a lovely solid clunk as you strike the ball, which goes flying in the air and lands within a couple of feet of where you aimed. Great shot! Unfortunately, you didn't allow for the slope. The ball starts rolling to the right, picking up speed as it goes and eventually travelling some twenty yards before it comes to a halt a good few feet into the rough.

It's easy to simply write something like that off as a bad attempt and conjure up some ever-elaborate invective with which to berate yourself, but don't forget that you made a 130-yard shot and landed it within a couple of feet of where you aimed. You matched your intention, albeit that your intention was misguided.

Suppose you had overhit it instead, shanking it horribly to the left, but it had somehow struck the tree, bounced clear of the rough and settled only a few yards from the pin. Would that have been better?

All too often we simply look at the result of something without considering whether we have matched our intention. It is in our interests to give ourselves credit and ingrain it in our brains when we have done something well and want to repeat it. The more often you match your intention, the more control you will have over whatever it is you are doing – and, as in the previous section, not become demoralized by a poor outcome, particularly when the outcome is beyond your control. Life throws up so many unforeseen obstacles and problems that it is beneficial at times to look at the result of an action and whether it matched its intention quite separately. Accuracy is not automatically rewarded, just as sloppiness is not always punished, but you should always try to make your actions match your intentions.

In cricket, so long as you're bowling at a good pace and you're bowling at the length you intended, then you have matched your intention. Just because a big hitter wallops it out of the ground doesn't make it a bad ball, and it is vital for the bowler to acknowledge this.

Shane Warne, the legendary Australian spin bowler, had, among the arsenal of both psychological and bowling weapons at his disposal, an ability to match his intention and recognize when he was doing so, regardless of what the batsman did. Such was his audacity, Warne would give the impression that even a bad ball was intentional, all part of a cunning plan, but for spin bowlers especially, it is a reality that they'll be smashed out of the park here and there. Warne wouldn't allow this to distract him – he'd keep probing and bowling, continuing to ask questions of the batsman.

This, of course, is where things get interesting in a game of cricket. If the bowler is matching their intention and bowling well and the batsman is equal to it, it's time to decide whether to change tactics. Pressure influences our decision-making and it takes a great deal of mental resolve to be able to judge objectively whether the intention is being matched and then separate this from the result. Bowlers change tactics all the time when trying to get the batsman out, but it is important to recognize when you are performing well under pressure and to realize that sometimes it might be worth persisting with the same tactics regardless of what the batsman is doing. If you do change tactics it is important that you are still able to match your intention now that you are approaching it differently.

It's tough to accept that sometimes doing the right thing produces the wrong outcome, I know, but when you adopt the no limits mindset you are, in truth, only in competition with yourself when it comes to learning and improving. It's true, if clichéd, that there's no shame in giving your all and being beaten by a better opponent; however, there *is* shame in not performing to the best of your abilities.

Empathy

Those who dare to teach must never cease to learn. That is the inscription on a wooden plaque that sits on the desk of Mark 'Gibbo' Gibson, chairman of the Australian PGA and a golf teacher – an appellation he prefers to 'instructor' – and, as his motto makes clear, a self-confessed student.

Learning, the ability to repeatedly get in the ugly zone and develop mastery of something, is a skill in itself and, equally, for any teacher, manager or coach, overseeing that learning is also a skill. While some technical expertise in your chosen field is obviously a prerequisite for any instructor, most teaching literature also emphasizes the importance of empathy with the person being instructed. And what better form of empathy is there than learning something new yourself?

Empathy with the learner should mean understanding what it takes to get ugly and master a new skill. It means experiencing all that angst and frustration and trying and failing and trying again. How can any coach, manager or teacher have empathy otherwise? It's easy to forget this – indeed, it was something I only discovered myself in 2007.

That year, I found myself wondering why some top rugby players couldn't perform basic kicking skills. It seemed so easy to me! I'd had the same experience during 2005–06 with England, when there was a high turnover of players in the squad. I'd start a training session with the mindset that it should be a straightforward morning and then, when it wasn't, I'd become increasingly impatient. *What on earth was the matter with these so-called internationals?*

There was nothing wrong with them – they were the best in the country. The problem lay with me: I had lost my empathy with the learning process.

It was then that I turned to Gibbo. I had always been interested in golf, both in its unique pressure environment for professional players and as a player myself; whenever an opportunity had arisen to play a round while on a rugby tour I had jumped at the chance and had become a pretty effective hacker in the process. But I did think to myself that I would love to learn to play this beautiful game properly.

Under Gibbo's tutelage, I started rediscovering my empathy with the learning process and I began to see the obvious similarities golf shared with kicking in rugby and penalty taking in football. Most importantly, I reacquainted myself with real angst and frustration, the pain of thinking I'd mastered a particular technique only to find it had slipped from my grasp when next called upon – of getting in the ugly zone. And, boy, was it ugly!

My experience in golf has made me an infinitely more effective coach in all sports. Sadly, such an empathetic outlook isn't universal among those whose job it is to develop others. A few years ago I delivered a 'No Limits' presentation to almost forty elite academy managers of a major national sports governing body in the UK. When I asked the room if anyone was learning anything new themselves, be it a musical instrument, a foreign language or a sport, I was greeted by silence. 'How can you empathize with the learner if you have no recent recollection of learning anything yourself?' I asked, to more silence.

Remember, it's never too late to pick something new up and start progressing.

The Silo Trap

In my experience, the organization of elite-level rugby is excellent in terms of delivery of information to players, but often fails to prepare them properly for the game. One of the reasons might be familiar to anyone working in business or education: a lack of joint planning, with individual departments too busy competing for time rather than working together.

The week of a Test match with an international rugby squad can be a fraught period. The specialist coaches all compete for player time and are then jointly in competition with the strength and conditioning coaches. The more time spent on strength and conditioning, the less is spent working on the game. During the World Cup 2011 campaign, particularly in the latter stages, I felt that there was too much time being spent on physical conditioning and not enough on working on skills under pressure. When it came to playing France in the quarter-final, England's play was littered with uncharacteristic mistakes, which eventually cost the team a place in the semi-final.

Perhaps you have experienced a similar conflict of interest between various departments yourself. It's a bit like allocating resources in a secondary school. Every teacher wants the best for the students in their own particular subject, which is not necessarily the same as the best for the students generally.

Before I started coaching full-time, I was a secondary school teacher at a large inner-city comprehensive, where I taught Commerce (a mixture of Economics and Business Studies). The pupils were not as highly motivated as I would have liked – a common complaint among many teachers – and they exhibited many of the factors that prevent people getting in the ugly zone that we've already discussed, not least self-esteem and peer influence.

One of the projects I devised for my students as part of their coursework was to put together a business plan to secure a bank loan. They had to explain how they would manage the business, give a forecast of future profits with justification for their accuracy – typical business-plan stuff. Many of the reports the pupils submitted made sound economic sense, but the English and presentation were sorely lacking. When challenged on this, the students would respond with a line many teachers will be familiar with: 'This is Commerce, not English, so what does it matter?' They had a point, in terms of their Commerce GCSE qualification, but as preparation for life after school they did not; in the real world a bank manager is likely to be put off by spelling mistakes and poor grammar and punctuation.

The GCSE English qualification was based in the main on coursework, with one of the pieces a project report with a reasoned rationale, so, after I approached an English teacher, together we constructed a project that would satisfy the marking criteria for both English and Commerce. This joint effort produced a piece of work much more relevant to life after school and, as a result, a much more efficient use of the students' time. It was a much more match-relevant piece of work, and the students were more motivated by doing something that spanned two subjects. Unfortunately, while the marks were much better than predicted, the English teacher and I were warned by the examination board not to do anything like that again in the future. They wanted the subjects to remain separate, each confined to its own silo.

Fast forward to my career in sport and this silo mentality becomes all too clear. Because of the influx of specialists, particularly in strength and conditioning, there is tension between the coaches and the specialists. I am certainly not against new and improving expertise – far from it – but I am concerned that more new elements foster and increase the pressures on each component, and consequently the silo mentality becomes stronger. A solution is not straightforward, but surely integrated planning and execution – be it in subjects at school or in the backroom staff at a rugby club – has to be part of it. But you can imagine the sticking points: who is in charge? Who do we blame if it all goes wrong? The irony is that, while we coach a team game in which we try to foster a culture of joint responsibility, as a group of teachers and coaches we are unable to do the same.

I see no reason why strength and conditioning work can't integrate with the preparation for other parts of the game. Why, when players are running up a hill ten times for fitness and power, can't they do it holding a ball? Why, each time they run down, ever-more fatigued, can't they do it while passing the ball along the line – practising a match-day skill while improving their endurance.

At one club side, I tried to get the players kicking into a crash mat against a wall between sets of heavy weights in the gym to improve their ball-striking skills. I don't think it lasted a week before the strength and conditioning team dumped the idea. Despite my protests that an environment in which the players were allowed to practise skills under the force of extreme fatigue, just as in a match, would be of great benefit, they didn't agree. Jonny Wilkinson, when he was in Cardiff on 24 May 2014, spent the morning kicking balls into a crash mat to get a feel and concentrate on the process – and then, in the afternoon, he led Toulon out to a resounding victory in the

European Cup final in the Millennium Stadium, without missing a kick.

In sport, the more we can integrate our approach to training and preparation, the more we can replicate match conditions. In the same way I believe that a more integrated approach to education, such as merging some aspects of an English and Commerce course, will prepare young people for the match conditions after school – real life. As coaches and teachers, we have a responsibility to see the needs of our own discipline within the landscape of the bigger picture – to put our egos to one side – so that the people we are coaching and the children we are teaching can perform at their best when the pressure comes on match day – or after school's out for ever.

Nothing to Fear but Fear (of Failure) Itself

As the final section in a chapter about managing learning, it seems fitting to return to our childlike selves. The first time we experience learning is with our parents, and how they support our performance is crucial. The way we see disappointment or failure is the litmus test of the 'mental environment' in which we develop, when the learning culture is set. Parents naturally want their children to be successful and happy. When, as children, we start playing, we are learning, and parents desperately want the learning to continue with enthusiasm and excitement.

If a group of children are playing kickabout in the park, perhaps the dads might join in. For the fathers this is playing with their children, to the youngsters it is learning: they mimic and explore. They'd likely get competitive as their game develops; they might even join a junior football club. It is the attitude at home – the culture being fostered – that is important: what is considered important about the football? Is it the social aspect, the enjoyment, the improvement, the physical activity? Or is it being selected for the team? If they're successful in this, what is the reaction? Is it: 'Well done for getting in the team'? Or 'Isn't it great that you have the opportunity to play in the team'? Is it: 'We really think you are improving and are pleased you're enjoying it'?

What is the reaction if the child doesn't make the team? If making the team isn't the be all and end all for the parents, if it's more about enjoyment and being excited about improving, it could go some way to leavening the disappointment. But if the child thinks their parents are likely to be disappointed, this could be a formative experience of outcome-related pressure for the youngster.

Most youth football teams, in the very early stages, are more about making sure all the children are playing and enjoying it, and efforts are made to include every child. Sooner or later – and in many cases too soon – the pressure and expectation will be that the better players get in the team and the rest don't. Not only this, but the nature of the game – learning new skills, playing without a definitive outcome (winners and losers) – all too often becomes submerged in the competitive brunt that encapsulates the adult game. The fun of the game, in children who are still developing their skills, becomes a burden of expectation: to get in the team and to win.

This approach to youth football in England is often compared unfavourably with that in other countries, particularly in the Netherlands, where youngsters are coached with an emphasis on fun and skill development on smaller pitches, before they play eleven against eleven on full-size pitches as they get older. Some progress is being made, with the English FA's Youth Development Review producing changes that are, according to their website, 'about a modern, child-friendly approach to youth football, challenging the win-at-all-costs mentality that is stifling development and enjoyment for young people. Working together with a proactive attitude, adults can help develop a better learning environment for young people, that puts their needs at the centre of the process.' But the sad fact is that many young players are squeezed out of participating in sports by a competitive, outcome-based culture too early.

Children develop and grow at different rates. An under-11 team would include a wide range of physical shapes, abilities, sizes and maturities – and that same group of players at the age of seventeen would be a completely different set of players physically. They would all have developed and matured at different rates, with their abilities and skills also progressing at different speeds. I have witnessed too many cases of children specializing too early in a sport and as a result giving up on all sorts of other opportunities. I have seen a ten-year-old signed, via his parents, for a professional club. When he was in the under-10s he was top scorer and a regular man-of-the-match, but by the time he was fifteen he was struggling to have anything like that kind of influence. He'd been prevented from playing rugby, cricket or athletics under pressure from his parents and the club – the kind of pressure that is extremely difficult for a teenager to deal with. At the age of seventeen he was discarded by the club after having left school at sixteen with nothing.

The challenge, then, is to keep a range of activities accessible and to find ways for youngsters to enjoy whatever interests them. No matter how promising they are at a particular sport or subject, a general approach to all available sports and activities should be maintained. People develop at different rates and, while few of us are destined to become world champions, the one thing we can all support is the enthusiasm towards continual learning, exploring and improving – whether it's in a sport or natural history or astronomy. Can you remember the exuberance with which you first approached these subjects?

It's up to us to allow young people to continue a childlike approach to learning. And it's an attitude we all need to recapture if we're to better ourselves – and improve our performance under pressure.

Principle 3: Managing Learning

The ability to manage learning rather than simply instruct or direct increases understanding and raises the potential level of performance.

Detailed instruction-based coaching often leads to confusion, which interferes with the ability to perform under pressure.

4. IMPLICIT-EXPLICIT BALANCE

4.

The Tip of the Iceberg

You're on the squash court. Sweat is pouring down your face, you're breathing heavily and the lights in the sports hall feel brighter than usual, as though they're piercing your eyes and simmering in your brain, where a dull headache is starting to form. You're down in the match and your opponent, a colleague from work you usually get on perfectly well with, is assuming the characteristics of a sworn enemy as she prepares to serve. Time seems to be slowing down . . . until the ball is struck and it seems to jolt forward as you mishit yet another shot and lose the point once again.

You've got some self-talk on the go: *Concentrate on the ball and win the next rally*. But the harder you try, the worse it gets: you scuttle round the court hopelessly, chasing shadows, desperate just to keep the rally going and hoping you can force an error. You lose point after point, trying ever harder in the process.

Now, with the game starting to feel beyond you and your body feeling unusually racked by the exertion, your mind is being hijacked. You're drowning in a deluge of destructive, interfering thoughts so that you can no longer do anything intuitively. You know you must hit the ball more cleanly, get in a better position to make the shot, get your leaden footwork right, but not only are you having to contend with these myriad technical aspects, your frustration, anger, doubt and humiliation are also threatening to bubble over. You can't stop thinking about the last rally, about what will happen if you lose this game – you're even starting to wonder if you can ever face working with your opponent again, you're so furious with her.

The pressure is really on. As you ready yourself to receive serve again, lost in your red mist, you wonder to yourself: *How can I dismiss this swarm of negative thoughts and emotions so that I can play as well as I know I am capable?*

Or, perhaps more likely: *How the hell do I win the next damn point?*

That One Simple Thought

In October 2014, in a large sports hall at St George's Park, the Football Association's training headquarters in Stoke, I, along with the England and Wales Cricket Board's (ECB) principal fast-bowling coach Kevin Shine, was making a presentation to a group of elite cricket coaches. The idea was to illustrate a more 'implicit' coaching style.

I illustrated this by helping Chris Taylor – an ECB fielding coach and keen amateur golfer – learn the low-punch shot in golf, something he had been trying to master for some time, even having lessons from PGA coaches. We had a cricket wicket laid across the floor with hanging nets at one end. About ten yards from the net we had set up a golf mat, like any you'd see at a golf driving range, and behind the mat was a TrackMan radar system, a must-have training tool for any professional golfer.

The vast array of technical data from the radar – such as club-head speed, dynamic loft and the like – was projected on to a large screen behind Chris, where all the delegates could see it; in front of Chris was an iPad, which showed only two pieces of data from the TrackMan: the projected height and the distance of the shot. Chris was only allowed to look at the information in front of him and we had agreed that, if he took a peek at the data behind him, he would have to pay for the session!

Chris started hitting some shots with a nine iron into the net and I asked him to note the ball height each time. The height started off at around ninety feet, before I started giving Chris some advice: that he should press his hands slightly further forward when he made contact with the ball to produce a lower flight. However, both the audience and Chris could see that in his subsequent shots he was still hitting too high.

I have seen this in many talented people I've coached: he thought he had got his hands forward as asked, but in the split second of the swing he went back to his original position. Verbal instruction often has this non-result.

I then set up a pair of cricket stumps as a 'gate' about five yards in front of the ball and asked him to start hitting his shots through it. The first went high, but the next one went through the gate and so did the following shots. Chris had adapted his swing because of the target. I then moved the gate another yard back and Chris reacted by leaning further forward into the shot, which decreased the dynamic loft and lowered the ball flight. After moving it forward again, Chris was hitting shots that were only getting up to around fifty feet high, with some even lower.

By introducing an external intervention, rather than just a verbal instruction, Chris was able to reframe his thinking into a single, explicit thought: *get the ball through the gate*. Rather than thinking through minor technical changes to the swing and grip, he was able to let his subconscious process take over as he delivered on that one specific task. Having the target right in front of him allowed him to see this clearly and left him with his mental key to execute his low-punch shot. Golf can be a simple game when we allow it to be.

You can experience something very similar without learning golf. If a friend asks you to throw a ball to them when they're standing a few yards away, the chances are you'd just throw it without even thinking about it. If they then moved back to a distance of, say, ten yards, you'd likely do the same – with the adjustment of the applied power, backswing and change in release point happening subconsciously. If you were then asked to throw the ball up higher you would adapt again; you wouldn't stop to consciously think about changing the swing and release point – this is all implicit. The key to the changes, the explicit thought, is simply the distance to the target and the height, much as the wicket was the stimulus for Chris to adapt his golf shot.

The reason we can do this, and that Chris was able to adjust his swing subconsciously, is because we've got so much practice in the bank. Growing up, we've played simple games of 'catch' and then moved on to the likes of rounders, and there are countless occasions when we'll have been asked to 'throw' something towards someone – be it an apple from the fruit bowl or an eraser in the classroom – so that all our practice has produced a skill that is well within our comfort zone, and whose mechanics have become procedural, subconscious thoughts. These are our well-practised motor skills that we can rely on without having to think about them.

US PGA golfer Ben Crenshaw spoke with real affection about his coach Harvey Penick, in the latter's *Little Red Video*, saying how Harvey wanted players to take 'dead aim', which meant picking out the smallest possible target, whether it was a spot on the green for a chip shot or a precise point on the fairway for a drive off the tee. Ben posed the question: 'Why is it that, when we hit a great shot in golf, we often try to work out the thoughts that were going through our head at the time so we can repeat it?'

The reality is that, for most of us, there is no explicit thought involved in such actions. We simply pick out the target and let the swing or throw or kick happen. And why is it that when our head is full of interference and thoughts about technique we don't play well? Because we forget to take dead aim. In fact, it is the single, engaging process of taking dead aim – really seeing that very small target in extreme detail – that helps to displace the potential interference and allows your subconscious to deal with the finer details of technique. The weight of your thoughts leans towards the implicit side, with just one explicit idea.

This is called implicit–explicit balance, and a good way to understand it is to think of an iceberg. The tip of the iceberg – the part visible above the water – represents conscious, explicit thought. The vast proportion of an iceberg is actually underwater: the subconscious, implicit mind. It is here that all the time spent learning how to swing, throw or whatever is lodged – all the work on technique and practice. This is called repair, and will be discussed in detail in the next chapter. For now, let's just say repair is working specifically on each part of the technique to create a strong and stable foundation that will withstand whatever pressure it is subjected to. Utilizing a single explicit thought – get the ball through the gate – then lets us tap into that solid, implicit iceberg – the swing mechanics, the sequencing – that lies in the subconscious.

The Trolley Dash

You drive to the small local supermarket and pull up outside on double yellow lines. You can see a traffic warden a couple of hundred yards down the road. Your task, should you choose to accept it, is to run in and buy a pint of milk, a bunch of grapes and a packet of cornflakes. Your time starts . . . now!

You would no doubt be able to complete this task pretty easily, assuming there wasn't a huge queue to navigate, and drive off before the warden was on to you. Congratulations, you have performed effectively under pressure.

What if we change the scenario? You're on the yellow lines with the traffic warden 200 yards away, but this time you have to pick up a bag of brown sugar, four chicken breasts, a box of washing powder, a litre of orange juice, unsalted butter, a packet of raisin bagels, a bag of spinach, a dozen eggs, a packet of cherry tomatoes and two tins of tuna in oil, as well as the items earlier. Still feeling confident?

It's likely that you'd either forget something or get a ticket or both. The less you have to remember, the easier it is to perform under pressure.

If you're unlucky enough ever to have assembled a piece of flat-pack furniture, you'll be familiar with the booklet detailing the components and the step-by-step instructions. What almost no one ever does is read the instructions from start to finish, attempt to absorb all that information in one go and then go off and try to put the thing together. Instead we use the instructions as cues and concentrate on each step, *looking only at the instruction relevant to the task at hand*. As each step is completed we move on to the next, using the information in bite-sized, manageable chunks. Of course, there's probably a screw or crucial piece missing, in which case, well, you have my blessing to handle that particular pressure situation as badly as you like.

So, back to your trolley dash: if you were instead given three items to find to start with and then regular updates on your shopping list announced over the supermarket tannoy as you entered the relevant aisle – 'Your next three items are . . .' – you'd be able to absorb and act upon these items in a much more efficient way. There wouldn't be any hesitation or paralysis as you frantically tried to remember if it was tuna in oil or in brine, and it's the same in any pressure situation: keep the amount of details to remember to the absolute essential minimum, because it won't get any easier to remember them when things get stressful. That's why when preparing for a test it's essential to concentrate on what you will be tested on, rather than attempting to memorize everything involved in the subject.

If you were a small business owner applying for a bank loan, you might not be expected to remember every single transaction in the history of your business without referring to a paper document, but you would be expected to know the important ones: recent turnover, profit and the like. We all know about the effect pressure can have on tasks we can usually perform easily, like some unfortunate budding entrepreneur struggling to remember their last year's turnover or profit in the face of derision from the Dragons on *Dragons' Den*. It may be that they genuinely haven't paid much attention to the figures, but it's more likely that they've over-prepared, and that these important figures have become lost among a plethora of data they have tried to memorize but will almost certainly not be asked for. Along with the multitude of other things they have to remember as part of their presentation, they've simply given their minds too much to do. Outside the 'den', they can no doubt readily recall these essential figures with ease, but when the pressure is on as they're delivering their pitch, it's a different story.

Too Much Information

We live in the information age. All manner of facts, figures and statistics are at our fingertips should we wish to access them. Want to know whether to take an umbrella with you to work today? That weather app on your phone will tell you the percentage chance of rain, not to mention the predicted temperature, wind speed and humidity. Want to know the best way to get back to your hotel in a hurry? Your map app will give you a variety of routes along with a range of transport options: walk, train, bicycle, taxi or bus.

Sport, in particular, is now home to an ever-increasing wealth of statistical information, traditionally rich food for the plentiful 'statto' types. Many games are overwhelmed with it. The language of football discussion has changed markedly in recent years, with pub talk now likely to include pass-completion rates, possession and the distance covered by individual players. It is as if the central tenet of the game – to score more goals than the opposition – has somehow changed. The likes of Arsène Wenger of Arsenal and Pep Guardiola, whose obsession with possession first at Barcelona and then Bayern Munich has played its role in making such stats *en vogue*, epitomize the image of football managers today, utilizing the wealth of data at their disposal to give their teams an edge.

So, with all this information at hand, wouldn't it be best to tool up with as much as possible? Isn't it a case that the more information you have, the better you'll perform? The answer depends on the individual.

Not that long ago I was working with three touring golf pros, all very different people and a range of ages. There was a marked variation in their ability to take on information and react to it productively. Player A needed very little information to play well – what some people are fond of calling a 'natural', rather than a product of his environment – but his ability to absorb usable information was limited and too much information had a dramatic negative impact on his ability to perform under pressure. Player B was able to take on more information, but he too had to be careful not to suffer from 'paralysis of analysis', particularly in regard to his swing. Player C had a deeper knowledge of his technique and was able to use more information, but this didn't necessarily mean player C performed any better than the other two.

There is no unequivocally 'best' way to use statistics. Some people need more detail to perform, some need to keep it simple and others prefer something in between. With extremely talented elite players, usually the less explicit the learning (the fewer facts and interventions), the more effective the learning tends to be. In other words, I'm championing having less but more relevant information.

Even player C types, who are able to absorb and use a lot of information, will still have a limit on the amount they can use efficiently. This particular player was given the opportunity to have a sophisticated video analysis done in the lead-up to a big tournament. Given his desire for knowledge and self-improvement, he jumped at the chance, but when the analysis was done, despite the operator identifying one or two areas that could potentially help his swing, the player – who had a very clear idea of what his swing should ideally be – spotted another few areas that he could also change. So, in the week of a big Tour event, there was so much going on mentally that on the first two rounds he played well below his capability and missed the cut. It was a classic case of paralysis by over-analysis.

If we go back to the example of Chris learning the low-punch shot earlier, he was given only two pieces of information, whereas the rest of the room had the whole arsenal to refer to. When it came to improving his shot, it was the case that he needed just one piece of feedback – the height – to know he'd succeeded.

Golf is a perfect example of a sport where, thanks to technology, a wealth of information can be gleaned from an act as apparently simple as a club striking the ball. There are a number of incredibly sophisticated analysis systems available which can produce a huge amount of data, but this information is of no use unless it is managed correctly. I use the already-mentioned Track-Man radar, which produces a vast array of technical data, all of which has its time and place – but that time and place most certainly is not in a player's conscious thoughts when they are striking the ball.

The key is to provide the information relevant to the task in hand. The TrackMan can be adjusted so that it supplies only certain pieces of information, specific to the particular practice being undertaken, so that the player can concentrate on committing to that part of the process without being distracted. In this respect, it is similar to putting that net three yards in front of a rugby kicker or putting stabilizers on a child's bicycle – with the outcome removed, it can't interfere with their thoughts.

Me, My Selves and I

The implicit–explicit balance so vital to performing under pressure can be compared with Timothy Gallwey's *The Inner Game of*

Tennis, in which he describes the two parts of our thinking – our two 'selves'. He describes them thus:

> *I found self 1 – the verbalising, thought-producing self – is a lousy boss when it comes to control of the body's muscle system. When self 2 – the body itself – is allowed to control, the quality of performance, the level of enjoyment and the rate of learning are all improved.*

If we return to your travails on the squash court at the start of the chapter, with your destructive thoughts and self-criticisms running wild, you asked: *How can I dismiss this swarm of negative thoughts and emotions so that I can play as well as I know I am capable?*

The key is to find something simple yet engaging to keep self 1 busy, losing it in an engaging process, so that self 2 is free to take over. For the squash court, I would suggest Gallwey's 'Bounce, hit', which involves you saying 'bounce' to yourself at the *precise* time the ball hits the ground and then saying 'hit' – again, to yourself, not to your opponent – at the moment you hit the ball with your racket. Through these simple conscious and exact thoughts, your attention should move to watching the ball and getting your timing right. You allow your subconscious mind to take over the technique involved in striking the ball.

Do Not Open the Folder

Technique in any task you attempt is important, but it shouldn't be in your conscious thoughts when performing under pressure. Thoughts about your technique are necessary when you learn and practise but not when you are executing a skill for real. The middle of your squash match is not the time or place to start thinking about the position of your elbow or how you're holding the racket.

One way of looking at it is to compare your mind to a

computer. Let's think of the desktop as being your consciousness and on it are folders for your subconscious with documents labelled 'Grip', 'Stance', 'Posture' etc. (all elements of the technique that support your process) within. For a game like squash, the folder would be labelled 'Feel' – what you know a perfect strike feels like – followed by one instructional process key. In the case of your squash match, let's use Gallwey's 'Bounce, hit'.

This is how everything should be when you're performing under pressure: the folder sits in plain sight on your desktop, labelled correctly with your conscious thoughts – 'Feel' or 'Bounce, hit' – and contains all the documents necessary for you to perform. Your preparation work is done and you'll be judged on the whole contents of the folder.

However, under match conditions the folder should be thought of as being like Pandora's box: it must not be opened. To do so would be akin to starting to edit a report after you'd handed it over as complete, or trying to change your sales pitch halfway through a presentation. On the squash court, with things going wrong and your mind running riot, you've opened documents like 'Grip' and 'Stance' and started to fiddle about with them and then your negative, self-critical thoughts come flooding on to the screen in the form of unwanted pop-ups. All of this inhibits your performance – slowing down your processor – and distracts you from the task at hand. If too many documents are opened at once, the system might even crash completely. You'll have 'choked'.

System Jam

The terms 'choking', 'freezing', 'quitting', 'icing', 'bottling' and 'the yips' are all expressions that have entered everyday use. They all describe pretty much the same thing: an inability to perform at the crucial moment or moments of a contest owing to anxiety.

The most famous examples of choking in the sporting world tend to involve an elite-level professional with victory in sight on the grandest stage of all suddenly losing his or her ability to execute skills that they had previously been using to great effect.

Think of Greg Norman, the Great White Shark, blowing a six-shot lead on the final round of the Augusta Masters in 1996, handing victory to Nick Faldo. Think of Jimmy 'the Whirlwind' White, the six-times snooker world championship finalist but no-time world champion, whose 1994 defeat hinged on missing a makeable pot on the black in the deciding frame to hand victory to Stephen Hendry. Think of Jana Novotna, who in the space of ten minutes went from the verge of 1993 Wimbledon champion to being the losing finalist against Steffi Graf. Think perhaps not of England football players taking penalties – we will come to them – but of Italy's Roberto Baggio, one of the greatest ever to have played the game and a regular scorer for club and country, blazing his decisive penalty over the crossbar in the shootout of the 1994 World Cup Final, having dragged his team there almost single-handedly.

These performers, no matter how unfairly, are sometimes cited as lacking the necessary 'mental toughness' to take the top prizes in sport. But it isn't just those painted as being mentally fragile who can choke. Can you think of a more psychologically focused athlete than John McEnroe? Even he was not immune to choking, as his 1984 French Open final against Ivan Lendl demonstrates: McEnroe, who was unbeaten all year, let slip a two-set lead after one of his famous temper tantrums, on this occasion with a noisy cameraman, and Lendl came back to take the crown.

I dislike the term 'choking'. It has negative, almost cowardly implications. Many excellent, heroic performers have been unfairly labelled as weak under pressure, often by those who could not even begin to comprehend the kind of stresses involved in performing at the pinnacle of a sport. As golfer Tom Watson says: 'A lot of guys who have never choked have never been in the position to do so.' And, in fact, it isn't mental fragility that causes choking at all; it's more like a lack of mental discipline, or a failure to organize one's thoughts when the pressure is on.

Choking occurs when the anxiety of the situation causes a player to become conscious of and unpick things that had hitherto been automatic – a well-practised motor skill like a golf swing, cue action or kicking technique. Subconscious thoughts start intruding, crowding the conscious mind, and I prefer to think of choking not as a sudden inability at a pivotal moment, but more as an overload of information that causes the sensory system to jam, just like the computer mentioned earlier. This is why I would like very much to replace the word 'choking' in our vocabulary with 'system jam'.

Once you start fiddling with stuff that had previously been automatic in the procedural memory in an attempt to regain your lost form, you find yourself in a real mess, as you are dealing not only with all the things that are always present in your conscious mind at pressure moments but also with the stuff that you would usually do without thinking – the subconscious actions you've done implicitly a thousand times before – and you suddenly find yourself unable to execute the skill automatically.

Of course, system jams aren't confined to elite-level sportsmen. A public speaker well practised in addressing colleagues in the office could end up mumbling at the floor at an international conference with an audience of thousands. A child who excels in school PE lessons could freeze when sports day comes around, performing for the first time in front of a crowd, with parents and peers looking on.

At its root, then, a system jam results from fear of failure. And nowhere does this fear manifest itself more than when an underdog reaches a potentially winning position. Having executed their familiar motor skills throughout the match or tournament, they're suddenly in a place they've never been before and haven't been able to prepare for. And once the expectation that they might, or even *should* win comes about, fear of failure can rear its ugly head and make them start to worry about that which should be automatic – Greg Norman's swing, Jimmy White's cueing action, Roberto Baggio's penalty technique.

In the next chapter, we'll talk more fully about the documents in the folder on the desktop, the 'repair' that belongs in your subconscious when performing a skill. But as for our conscious thoughts that label the folder, how do we come to know what 'feel' is right? And how can we best use this thought to help us perform under pressure?

Top Pocket

It was a cold winter's evening in Edinburgh and the converted church hall was alive with the sound of judo players crashing on to mats under the force of an opponent's throw. After each throw, the player responsible would turn towards head coach Billy Cusack – who was in charge of the judo coaching team for the 2008 Olympics – and shout out two seemingly random numbers.

'Minus one and plus a half,' shouted one.

'Two and minus one,' came another.

Euan Burton – gold medallist at the 2014 Commonwealth Games – threw a player effortlessly over his shoulder and, after a moment's thought, called out: 'Zero, zero – double top pocket!'

Billy Cusack nodded, then turned to 2006 European Champion Sarah Clark, whose opponent had just been dispatched to the mat. 'Zero, zero . . . I think,' Sarah said.

'Are you sure?' asked Billy. 'How did it *feel*?'

'I didn't feel anything,' said Sarah. 'It was as if she were weightless.'

'Then you're right.' Billy smiled. 'Zero, zero – great throw.'

The casual observer might wonder why on earth players were shouting out seemingly random numbers, and they might wonder even more once they realized what the numbers were: the judo players were working on the feel of each throw – and, perhaps more oddly, they were scoring their own throws.

The Top Pocket system is, much like the C–J concept, one of the tools I have developed for my coaching kit, and again it can be applied across a host of disciplines: I use it when coaching rugby kicking, football, cricket and golf, as well as judo. In fact, for any sport that involves any striking or contact. And, also like C to J, while its roots and base applications are in the sporting world, the philosophy behind it can be – and indeed already is – applied to all of our lives.

In the Top Pocket system, a player labels each kick, bowl, shot or throw with a numerical value. The score is based entirely on how the action feels to you. In football it's not as black and white as a good strike being great and a mishit, disaster; there are various grades for the mishit. This numerical value describes the energy waste, so that zero is a perfect strike or throw, with no energy lost, and a plus or minus figure describes the amount of energy wrapped or leaked. The bigger the number, the greater the energy wasted. The system is a tool for self-improvement: it is impossible to compare one player to another when it measures something so subjective that only the person experiencing it knows how it feels.

Imagine I asked you to kick a ball and then tell me how it felt off your foot. 'OK,' you might say, 'but not great.' Then I'd ask you to kick it again and you might say that you felt this shot was better. So, then I'd ask you to tell me what the difference was with the first one: did you pull it a little (perhaps wrapping your foot around the ball and sending it left, if you're right-footed) or did you slice it (catch the ball too far on the left side and send it right)? If it's the former then we can say you've had an energy wrap and it's a plus value. With the latter, when the ball escapes right – a slice – it's an energy leak, which will be given a minus value. A zero would be your feeling of an effortless straight and true shot. What's important is your comparison, so that you start to become much more aware of what it is you've done through feel. On some occasions and for some skills – such as a footballer hitting a curling cross – a slight energy wrap is deliberate to add spin, so a plus score can be desirable.

In judo the players worked from their own kinaesthetic map, based on their balance and energy application. The easier the throw, the lower the number the player calls out. Billy Cusack was enthusiastic about the system, saying: 'Although we have only been doing it a while, the impact has been dramatic in that it gets the individual to take much more responsibility for their technique.'

And that, in its essence, is the major benefit of Top Pocket. It gives us responsibility for developing our own technique, which encourages us to understand more about exactly what we're doing. Once we start to want to understand more – how that throw *felt* and what we can do to improve it – then it encourages our negatively weighted mind to see the positives of persevering without any guarantee of success. And if we can do this, we will more readily commit to the ugly zone (see Chapter 3).

As Euan Burton says: 'It makes the sessions much more mentally demanding. Rather than just throwing ten or twenty reps of a particular throw, you have to really think about each one and adjust when it's not a zero and work out which way you have to make the adjustment – getting a little closer, perhaps, or keeping the distance so your opponent goes over your shoulder, rather than the base of your neck. It's tough but it does make you think.'

We're not used to quantifying feel, despite touch being one of our five senses. Unless we can objectively see or hear something, we're not willing to trust it. But using Top Pocket allows me to tap into this element in a language both the player and I can understand. Ultimately, as a coach I have to work from the player's map of reality in order to empathize fully with them and, as the player will be doing a lot of their work on their own, it's a useful tool for them to measure and engage with their learning. In a match situation, things don't always go according to plan; an improved understanding will give the player a better chance of knowing exactly what has happened – and what they can do about it. This tool is also the ultimate in implicit learning, as when you simply concentrate on the feel of the strike, everything else – the mechanics and all the technical stuff surrounding it – is relegated to your subconscious.

The inevitable criticism I hear levelled at this system is that the coach has to surrender the assessment to the player. 'How do they know what a minus one really is?' they might ask. But it actually requires trust in the player; for coaches, it means letting go of some control and putting our egos to one side. It can be extraordinarily empowering for anyone to take a more active part in their own development, and self-assessment is employed by all manner of industries outside sport, where pressure is just as powerful a force.

Don't Fight the Feeling

For those working in psychology healthcare – that is, treating people suffering from depression, anxiety and other disorders – self-assessment is a powerful tool for patients. After all, this is a part of healthcare that is entirely built upon how you feel.

When someone is referred by their GP to a specialist psychology service, they are usually initially assessed through a process of, among other things, self-appraisal, when they are asked to rate their mood, as well as other things – such as suicidal or self-harming thoughts – to ascertain the severity of the condition, the likelihood of the patient being in danger and the best course of treatment. For very serious problems all manner of treatments and medications are used, but for a non-life-threatening case of depression a patient might see a psychologist once a week. Here, self-assessment is again a vital tool, as patients are usually asked to complete a questionnaire when they arrive for an appointment. These usually comprise statements such as, 'I have felt tense, anxious or nervous over the last week' with a sliding scale of answers from 1 (never) to 5 (always). These scores are used to help assess the patient's condition and measure their progress, so that someone regularly ticking a 5 at the start of treatment who gets it down to a lower number has clearly made progress.

Of course, self-appraisal isn't used in isolation. Trained psychologists and doctors also talk to their patients and make their own assessments, and there is some evidence to support the idea that patients 'overstate' their wellbeing in order to please the person treating them. But they are nonetheless an invaluable aid to getting patients to spend a moment assigning a tangible, numerical value to how they feel about various aspects of their lives. Clinical anxiety or depression is usually rather more serious than run-of-the-mill performance anxiety, and I certainly would not compare my work to the difficult and highly pressured environment doctors, psychologists and psychiatrists operate in, but if the NHS can see the benefit in using self-assessment of feeling as a tool, then surely it is an approach we can use in our own lives.

In business, of course, it is already used, particularly in staff appraisals: 'How do you feel this last six months have gone?' Some companies ask their staff to rate their own performance on a scale of 1 to 10, or terrible to excellent. Again, it's a common complaint that these numbers might seem reductive, but surely the benefit is that the person at the heart of it is giving thought to their performance and communicating their feelings.

When we're under pressure, our minds can be attacked by unhelpful thoughts, our anxiety can get the better of us and it can become difficult to gauge an outcome accurately. Our subjective judgement might be way off and we might feel something has been a disaster that has actually gone perfectly well. This is the 'dentist effect' striking again, and just a few small adjustments – if they *feel* significant – can make all the difference.

It is, however, still worth taking stock of how you feel when you attempt anything under pressure, maybe even marking it out of ten, and then look at how it goes next time and the time after that, so you can build comparisons and see how you're progressing. You might have started a new job in a pub, working behind the bar. You've done several quiet shifts but never a Friday or Saturday night before, and now you've been moved to working every Friday night, when the pub is packed. How do you feel it went the first time, when the orders were flying in and you struggled to remember the drinks and you could hardly hear a thing because it was so loud and drunk people don't make a lot of sense? When your conscious thoughts were overwhelmed with 'How do I make that drink?' and 'Am I even up to this?' What about the second time, and the third? What would the perfect shift feel like?

The truth is that, as we get better at something, skills like how to pour a perfect pint, use a till swiftly and expertly swerve a drunken punter become relegated to our implicit memory, and the more we learn, through the methods offered in this book, to disperse our emotive, self-doubting thoughts, the better we are able to judge our own performance. That is why I trust sportspeople, with their hours of deliberate practice, to tell me what they feel is a perfect hit,* in the same way that the NHS trusts their patients to tell them how they feel. After all, who's had more practice at being you than you?

---

* In 2007, as part of a pilot British Olympic Association project, I was working with golfer Melissa Reid, who now plays on the Ladies European Tour. Mel was being fitted for a new set of golf clubs, so she was using a TrackMan, which would record the 'smash factor' scores – the mathematical relationship between club-head speed and the resulting ball speed – though she wouldn't see them, and we needed a perfect shot to take as a base reading. Mel started hitting and she was registering very high smash factor scores. But each time she hit it, she didn't feel it was quite right, giving me negative Top Pocket scores. Finally, she hit one, turned round and beamed. 'That was it – a zero.' I looked at the smash factor and it was her highest value yet: her subjective feeling had corresponded exactly with the machine's objective readings.

Nothing to Fear, Not Even Fear Itself

As your attempted trolley dash earlier demonstrated, when there is too much explicit information for our minds to absorb, and the implicit–explicit balance tips too far the wrong way, our performance declines. However, when we are faced with a decision or a challenge, many of us would prefer to arm ourselves with as much information as possible, assuming that it would better insulate us against the possibility of failure. But if we return to an earlier example, when you're late and lost in an unfamiliar city, would your smartphone's map, with its three different walking routes and various alternative forms of transport, each with its own options (standard taxi or Uber? Should you take this train line or the other?), allow you to make a quicker or more effective decision than, say, simply hailing a passing cab? Perhaps, given an abundance of time, it would allow you to pick the most effective one, but you're late, remember, you're under pressure. The most effective decision is one that is made quickly.

Now, this should be a question that can be quickly answered. Which would you say was the more difficult to master: skateboarding or playing golf? Or, to put it another way: what is more complicated, hitting a golf ball or balancing on a piece of wood with little wheels while barrelling over ramps and rails? One way to measure this might be to consider how many manuals and instruction books have been written in the last ten years on each subject. Unsurprisingly, the golfing publications dwarf those on skateboarding. In fact, 'dwarf' doesn't begin to describe the disparity.

If we wanted to be overly simplistic about the physics of it, golf is basically a game in which a club is swung towards a ball with its face moving towards the target at impact. If you were to write a book on skateboarding in the same manner in which a golfing manual is written, it would be as thick as a telephone directory. It would have to include weight distribution, moments of inertia, centrifugal force, friction, range and types of suspension, wheelbase width, centre of gravity, turning circles . . . it would be monstrous. Yet people do learn to skateboard and some become extremely proficient in it, as a quick search on YouTube or a walk past a local skate park will confirm. So, without these volumes of information available to them, how do skateboarders do it?

At the start of the previous chapter, I talked about my friend's golf lessons. He'd spent several sessions learning about the theory behind playing – plenty of explicit learning – but hadn't even hit a ball yet. This isn't an uncommon approach in golf. The game has a culture of teaching vast amounts of theoretical knowledge, often cloaked in confusing language, at least to the beginner, about open and closed club faces and plenty of *what not to do*. The whole undertaking is riddled with potential failure. It's this approach to learning, with an expectation to absorb lots of complicated explicit information, that makes golf seem so difficult. How about just hitting the ball?

In skateboarding, there is no failure. Skateboarders celebrate falling off – they call it 'wiping out'. They don't need a library of coaching manuals and expensive lessons with a pro, or to understand the maths and science behind their board speed or jumping angle, because they do their learning implicitly. They try something and, if it doesn't work, they don't turn to a coach or manual – they try it again, making the necessary adjustments according to how it went wrong and what they think they need to do differently until they get it right. They work through *feel*. Their feedback is immediate and visceral: if they fall off, it hurts. They don't spend hours dissecting their foot position, wondering if that was the issue. They're already up and trying again.

Granted, most skateboarders start young, so they have on their side the childlike approach to learning and getting in the ugly zone. But it is the whole culture of skateboarding that makes it such a perfect example of implicit learning. You can't fear failure if there's no failure to fear in the first place. Skateboarders, with their jeans ripped at the knee, embrace wiping out, celebrating where they go wrong. Could you imagine a golfer talking in the same way?

'I was on the eighteenth hole, about ninety yards out. I took a pitching wedge, swing was pretty good . . . but I really thinned it, and the ball shot past the flag and straight through the window of the clubhouse behind the green! Apparently, the ball bounced off the bar, smashing a load of drinks lined up in the process and the barman slipped in the spilt alcohol, crashed into the club secretary and they both landed on the floor in a heap. They're already talking about barring me from the course, but do you know what really upset me? The ball had settled on the club president's desk down the hall. It was a great lie – with the window open it was only twenty yards to the hole – but they wouldn't let me take the shot!' Gnarly.

The skateboarder learns quicker and with less information than the golfer, even though skateboarding is more complicated than golf. They do this because they have reframed failure as simple cause and effect and they haven't overloaded their brains with too much explicit theoretical information: their learning is implicit. A culture – a school, an organization, a sports team – that can reframe failure as part of a necessary facet of development can allow people to grow more freely, to use trial and error as a means of progression. Fear of failure can dramatically reduce a person's potential level of performance, increasing their anxiety and forcing them to play safe when making decisions rather than having the confidence to try something new – or something again, if they have failed at it before.

The golfer is led by the belief that more information will lead to improved performance, or at least less failure, as the avoidance-motivated individual might say. And it's not just in golf where this attitude prevails. We carry this with us to the workplace, where we imagine we can't be too prepared in terms of information; when we're late and lost in an unfamiliar city and we consult our smartphones; or when we worry about our health and decide to Google our symptoms and arm ourselves with a wealth of worrying information.

But as the skateboarders demonstrate, there is a great deal of benefit to be gleaned from the implicit approach: having a go at something, failing at it and trying again, making the adjustments necessary. Reading a manual on the intricacies of skateboarding or having classroom-style lessons seems absurd to us, yet doing the same for golf seems normal. But arming yourself with all the information in the world isn't going to insulate you from failure. 'Failure' is a natural part of any learning or practising of a skill, and only by accepting this and embracing it, instead of fearing it can we hope to take risks and improve. This is the ugly zone, where great progress happens.

The key, then, is to develop the right implicit–explicit balance. Information has its place, of course, and the right amount of relevant information is a requisite to improvement. But if we overload our minds with too much explicit instruction and thought it will inhibit us when we are learning and overwhelm us when it comes to performing under pressure. Our systems will struggle and, as the pressure mounts, eventually jam, our conscious minds overloaded with too much information.

So, when it comes to performing under pressure, we need to have our relevant information – our feel, our 'bounce, hit', our dead aim – to fully engage our conscious minds and the vast expanse of our well-practised, implicit skills packed tightly under the waterline, strengthening our icebergs.

Principle 4: Implicit–Explicit Balance

The more (irrelevant) explicit information provided, the more we interfere with our ability to perform under pressure.

5. BEHAVIOUR

5.

Big-Match Mentality

Dinner time in the Williams household. Mrs Williams is displaying all the organizational skills of an air-traffic controller at Heathrow as she marshals her three children through this most chaotic of mealtimes. Twelve-year-old Jimmy has just returned from football practice after school and eight-year-old Gillian is itching to get back to her cartoons, while Tom, the baby of the family at only thirteen months old, is doing his best to commandeer Mum's attention as he wields his food-laden spoon with reckless abandon. At this stage in his learning, Mum is happy with anything that lands south of his nose.

Jimmy and Gillian are talking over one another, each relaying different stories about their day, as Mum pulls off the difficult trick of appearing to give each her undivided attention while she expertly manages Tom's learning, gently guiding the spoon towards his mouth when required. A superb display of intense multitasking under pressure. Every time Tom gets it to his mouth unaided, she gives out an enthusiastic, 'Well done!' and he beams excitely back at her.

If we wanted to couch it in management terms or coaching language, Tom is on a 'cutlery handling micro skills-development programme'. This is where it all starts, on the high chair with the plastic bib as the catching trough. Mum is providing the positive reinforcement, leaving him in no doubt whatsoever when he's got it right. As time goes by, he becomes more proficient, the food all over his face a thing of the past as he progresses to a fork and spoon. He's able to stab solid bits of food and chart a course directly for his mouth with greater frequency. He's hacking his way through that forest, making a path to walk down.

Not only does Tom have deliberate physical instruction from Mum, but he also has constant training input from those around him, particularly his brother and sister, whose food-management skills are now advanced – their food disappearing without a trace into their mouths with every forkful.

Tom is essentially receiving training in manual dexterity, much like a dentist or surgeon training for a delicate procedure. As a result of repeated, deliberate practice and improving control, meat is introduced to Tom and, eventually, a knife so that he can cut it up himself. The plastic catching trough is replaced by a standard cloth bib and later just a napkin. Eventually, he comes out of the high chair to take his seat at the table with the adults, his implements – knife, fork and spoon – mere instruments in the hands of his growing skills. The intervention from Mum subsides; the expectation that he will be proficient grows.

Now, thirteen years later, Tom is at a grand family luncheon, with uncles and aunts and cousins and grandparents in tow, at a suitably fancy restaurant. All the adults are in their Sunday best, with the children, a couple of whom would now consider themselves adults too, immaculately turned out. The pressure to behave correctly, to demonstrate excellent table manners, to do the family proud, is on.

The first course goes without a hitch, polite conversation and all the food on target, despite the occasion making Tom more aware of his table manners than usual, forcing some of his subconscious, implicit actions up into his conscious thoughts. The mains arrive, with Tom having ordered the steak – after all, he is almost a man now. As the conversation flows at the table, with Jimmy regaling his grandparents with tales of his new job while, all too familiarly, Gillian vies for attention with her stories of university life, Tom eyes the thick slab of meat surrounded by a medley of vegetables on his plate. *They even have a special knife for it*, he thinks. *Maybe this wasn't such a good idea after all.*

Armed with the tools for the task, he prods his fork into the steak and begins to cut – to no avail. So then he starts sawing, but when that isn't effective, he begins to apply more pressure. Progress is still slow, so Tom, caught in the moment and with his perception of the occasion, the need for best behaviour narrowing to a point of almost extinction, he raises himself in his seat to apply more pressure and change the angle of his blade upon the stubborn steak.

As the tussle on his plate heats up, those around him continue talking, oblivious to the drama unfolding. And then, suddenly . . . disaster! The knife skids violently off his plate, and Tom falls forward into his food, sending meat across the table, scattering peas, carrots, broccoli – and toppling the bottle of red wine, flooding the table and drenching Mum's pristine white dress. In the midst of gasps and the beginnings of a mirthful smile across the lips of his brother, Tom's mum looks at him and hisses: 'That is *not* the way to behave at the table!'

My question is this: when did Tom's skill of using a knife and fork actually become a learned behaviour? Clearly, it started as a skill-learning programme, but under pressure at the table it became far less implicit and it's fair to say that Mum would label it a misbehaviour. Perhaps the coach's response would be: 'Great work with your grip on the fork, but be careful with over-recruiting on the knife at that angle – you might cause an accident.'

Making a Splash

A light drizzle of rain provided some welcome relief on a warm day on the Gold Coast in Queensland, Australia. I had a day off from coaching so thought I'd try swimming with the sharks at Sea World. Unfortunately, hundreds of others thought the same and, with the queue endless, I wandered off towards the dolphin show.

The dolphins were hugely impressive, swimming with great speed and then shooting out of the water to do two or three somersaults before splashing down. Two dolphins would swim together like a pair of organic water skis for the trainer to stand on. They would fetch a ball, balance it on their noses then push it back to the trainer waiting on the side. Later, two dolphins would come out with a trainer standing on each of their heads and the animals would catapult them out of the water a good fifteen feet in the air, before gravity returned them to the water. It was an incredible show, but it got me thinking: how did the dolphins learn these skills? And how did they get to be so good?

I asked the security guard who cleared out the crowd for the next show if I could stay and watch again. Reluctantly, she agreed. The second time was equally impressive, with the full repertoire of somersaults, water-skiing, retrieving balls and catapulting trainers out of the water, but I noticed that it was not exactly the same as the first. The dolphins leapt to incredible heights, but they were not consistent: sometimes they'd do two somersaults, sometimes three. The choice seemed random. I was intrigued, so when the show finished and I sheepishly asked if I could stay for the next, the guard shot me a slightly puzzled look and told me I could, but it would be the last performance of the day.

The third show was just as good again and the crowd lapped it up with heartfelt 'oohs' and 'aahs' and rapturous applause, but again the inconsistency was there. By now I needed answers: if the dolphins sometimes react randomly, what is stopping them from just swimming off and doing their own thing?

When the familiar guard arrived to usher me away, I asked if I could meet the person in charge of training the dolphins. Her face said, 'What on earth is with this guy?' but her mouth said, 'I'll see what I can do – but I can't promise anything.' She walked off and after a few minutes returned with a guy she introduced to me as Chris Macintyre.

Chris was the head of dolphin training and meeting him had a dramatic impact on my coaching philosophy. He showed me round the facilities behind the scenes and introduced me to the other trainers, while he explained the challenges they faced in training the dolphins and, surprisingly – at least to someone like me more used to imagining the friendly mammals of wildlife documentaries – informed me that they often fight among themselves in the pens. A few of the dolphins had bite marks from such confrontations. Chris and I spent a good couple of hours chatting about our respective professions and soon saw similarities in what each of us did for a living. He made me an offer I couldn't refuse: to come in and watch the trainers work with the dolphins in the morning.

The trainers each had their own specific dolphins to work with and training sessions were conducted in the same pool in which the paying public watched them, with the sessions coming to a close when the dolphins were signalled to swim through a gate and into their pens. The sessions were very well organized and it was a real education to witness at first-hand such patience and consistency.

Unlike training a toddler to use a fork by example, this was the ultimate in behaviour training. You can't make a dolphin mimic your actions, nor can you manipulate their bodies so they feel the correct movement, as you would Tom's hand with a spoonful of yoghurt. Indeed, the dolphin trainers used the word 'behaviour' to describe the response of the mammals when they gave a signal – it could be the wave of a hand or a short blast from a whistle – which might be to swim away and do a couple of somersaults or to collect a ball and bring it to the trainer. If its behaviour corresponds with the given signal, the trainer will leave the dolphin in no doubt by rewarding it, either through tone of voice, a pat on the head or with a small fish from a food pouch.

If the behaviour is wrong, however, the dolphin is 'ignored' by the trainer, who adopts a specific pose: standing upright, hands on hips (making sure there is no movement towards the food pouch), with one foot back and the other forward, its sole just over the edge of the pool. After a short while the dolphin, expecting a reward for its behaviour, will start to become agitated, squawking and nudging the trainer's foot. This is a crucial point in the dolphin's learning. The trainer doesn't budge and then, after a sufficient period of time has elapsed, they make the signal again to see what behaviour the dolphin responds with, ignoring the dolphin again if it is wrong. This process is repeated with the same outcome until the dolphin gets it right, in which case everything changes: the trainer becomes animated and enthusiastically makes a fuss of the dolphin, and perhaps feeds it from the pouch.

The fundamentals of dolphin training involve absolute consistency, incredible patience, staging (one piece of learning at a time), ignoring failure, enjoyment – and a big show of celebration when it's right. Most of all, it demands a great deal of discipline from the trainer. Any of this sound familiar? The similarities with teaching, coaching and management, and preparing ourselves to perform under pressure, are there, which is why, when Chris showed me the 'bible' of animal training, he pointed specifically to Karen Pryor's laws of shaping. Karen Pryor is an expert in the field of animal behaviour whose work with dolphins in the 1960s pioneered new methods of positive-reinforcement training. I have listed the ten laws she formulated below, along with my own comments on how each is more widely applicable to our own two-legged species.

Pryor's Ten Laws of Shaping

1. Raise criteria in small increments. By using successive approximations you will set the animal up to succeed.
   This is the basis of the 'no limits' mindset, which focuses on improvements at the margin of the components of our perform-

ance. The emphasis is improvement based on previous self. So often we fall into the trap of basing our improvement on other people's level of performance – something that we cannot control.

2. Train one criterion at a time. Keep your goals clear and remember the concept of black and white. When we train a dolphin to give us its tail so that we can take a voluntary blood sample there are multiple criteria. The dolphin must allow us to touch its tail, then hold its tail; it must remain calm, allow lengthy touching, accept pressure on the tail and eventually accept the insertion of a needle. These are just a few of the steps, each with its own criterion. We must be careful not to overwhelm an animal with too much all at once.
   To be more effective we should base our coaching, teaching and management on the performance level of the individual and specifically work at their margin. This will require planning and a clear understanding of exactly where that person is at that precise moment of time.

3. Vary reinforcement before moving to the next stage. Although we do not recommend that new trainers use a fully variable schedule of reinforcement until they gain experience, this is still an important rule. Reinforcement can be varied in many ways, including varying magnitude of reinforcement, type of reinforcement or requiring longer duration or repetition of the behaviour being trained.
   When someone is successful make sure they are in no doubt that they know they have succeeded. But try to match your reward to the challenge. If it was something that you would have expected to be successful, based on the level of difficulty and the experience and skill required, you must still reinforce that success. In coaching and teaching we tend to make assumptions that people know when they have performed correctly. If this continues we are in danger of drawing attention only to mistakes. Inadvertently we are reinforcing the very parts of the performance we want to avoid.

4. Relax old criteria when introducing new criteria. When an animal is being introduced to something new, it is not unusual for an animal to fail to meet all previously learned criteria. This is acceptable at first.

   Be aware that learning something new could have, in the beginning, a detrimental impact on a previously mastered skill. If you were trying to develop a different impact point in a golf swing and you had good posture at address before learning the change, it may well be that the posture would initially be worse than before as the player's attention would be totally fixed on the new impact position.

5. Plan ahead. Have a training plan/path in mind and know the eventual goals.

   Vital if we are to be at our most effective in managing learning. This requires a deep knowledge of the person we are training – we should take time to question and listen, rather than going straight in with our instruction.

6. Don't change trainers in midstream. For consistency it is not wise to have different people training the same behaviour.

   Consider teaching within a Western education system. Initially, very young children usually have the same teacher for all subjects. As they get older and academically more 'skilful', more teachers are introduced for different subjects. Towards the higher level they will probably have a specialist for each subject.

7. If a plan doesn't work, change the plan. Training is a dynamic process; so don't be afraid to change the plan if needed.

   Those who tell people WHAT to do will be less effective than those who manage learning by finding out HOW people can do something and the learner may become confused and frustrated – and give up. Or, in a professional environment, become 'expert' at hiding the deficiency.

8. Don't stop a session gratuitously. Stay focused, don't get distracted and don't end a session without a reason.
   The most effective coaches and teachers always have an awareness of the learner's state and it's their judgement (based on experience and emotional intelligence) as to when and how they should end the learning session. I have always used the benchmark of what I want their expectation to be for the next session – and worked from that.

9. Regress when behaviour deteriorates. Animals can forget or get confused. Taking a few steps backwards can refresh their memory and get them back on the right track.
   We should not make assumptions about prior learning. Often going back a few steps will reinforce the skill and understanding as well as providing both a great opportunity to draw attention to success and specifics within the process to reinforce the achievement.

10. End on a positive note. Keep training fun. Don't end a session if the animal is frustrated; end with success.
    When you are ending a session finish with great success. When I am working with international rugby goal kickers we try to finish with a great shot to go to bed with – a kick you could dream about and visualize in the next game. You can do the same in meetings: finish on something positive so everyone at least has the opportunity to leave the room feeling good – and perhaps they'll bring that energy to the start of the next meeting.

Fundamentally, Pryor's laws of shaping require a coach or trainer to be consistent in their response to their subject's – in this case a dolphin's – behaviour; the only action the trainer can initiate is to either accept or reject the behaviour, which reinforces that which we want to repeat and discards that which we don't. And, at a basic level, when we're managing or teaching people, that is exactly what we're doing. We should be making a big deal out of getting something right, not getting it wrong.

After my day at Sea World, Chris asked if I'd like to get involved for a few days and work with one of the dolphins. As I've already said, it's vital to keep learning new things if we're to teach, so how could I refuse?

As far as I can gather, Gemma the dolphin and I got on well. Chris guided me through the repertoire of signals – not unlike a mother guiding a spoon towards her child's mouth – and Gemma responded impeccably. She fetched the ball and dribbled it back with her forehead; she would swim off at pace around the pool, executing two somersaults and then returning; and my personal favourite was when I stepped back and raised my hand up high then waved it down to the floor and she leapt out of the water and skidded on her belly to my feet.

What was interesting was how easy it was to imagine that I was developing a relationship with Gemma. When I was talking to her, I was looking for an empathetic response in her actions, even just a subtle tilt of her head. When we're working with someone, we're much more effective when we know they have understood our communication.

It reminded me of the time I was working with the England polo squad. After a lot of work practising and turning on a Swiss ball the players had to transfer that 'feel' to their actions in the saddle. As I was addressing the six mounted players in front of me, I began to realize that I'd come over a bit Dr Dolittle, as I had, in fact, been addressing twelve pairs of eyes and looking for comprehension in all of them, including the horses'.

Working with Gemma the dolphin reinforced some of the ideas I've already mentioned, most notably that of positive reinforcement. Leadership guru Ken Blanchard's *The One Minute Manager* books suggest that to have the greatest impact on someone's ability to reach their full potential, it's necessary to catch them doing something right. As the dolphin trainers showed by rewarding their charges every time they did something right, and Mrs Williams demonstrated in her encouragement for Tom every time he landed his spoon home, positive reinforcement will encourage and produce the right behaviour. Whenever I see a player make a mistake in training and the coach bellows abuse across the pitch, I think of the behaviour model of reinforcing what you want to repeat and ignoring that which you don't and wonder what the chances are that they will reach their potential.

Pressure Practice

Those training the dolphins would say that they are coaching or 'shaping' the animal's behaviour, while baby Tom at the start of the chapter was undergoing a regime of both technical and behavioural coaching. But 'behaviour' has far greater implications than merely as a model for training and learning, and my interest has been piqued over the years by how coaching or teaching preparation and skills acquisition relate to match conditions. 'Match' obviously describes game day for sportspeople, the pressure-intense environment for which they prepare, but it's just as applicable to us all: for Tom, it was the big family dinner. For you, it could be anything from a job interview to entering a local *Great British Bake Off*-inspired competition. I've witnessed a looming disconnect between the way people practise or prepare for an event and what they are required to do when they perform in the event itself.

If we compare someone's actual behaviour in match conditions with how often they attempt to replicate that behaviour when practising, the disconnect is all too clear to see. The dolphins practise with the same trainer and in the same pool as on match day, when they perform in front of the public. They do the same things in training as when they perform. Compare that with a snooker player practising a specific shot again and again. Eventually, they'll get it right every time. But the match comprises a series of single shots, all different, often with a substantial break between. They get only one chance to make each shot.

It's the same for a pianist preparing for a recital. They can play the piece over and over again while they're practising, but when it comes to the real thing, they won't get a second chance at it.

Practice, it is said, makes perfect, and it's true that repetition helps in acquiring a specific skill. But possessing a skill counts for little if it can't be performed when it matters. The key to effective practice, then, is to make it purposeful. Of course, repetition has its place, but in order to be effective, practice must also reproduce match conditions as closely as possible.

Having wrestled with the challenge over a number of years, I eventually created a system of purposeful practice management, in which there are three elements. I call them **repair**, **training** and **match**.

Repair

Let's jump ahead twenty years from Tom's disastrous steak dinner and drop in on him at thirty-three. Neither the restaurant debacle nor his skill-development course in cutlery utilization appear to have left any lasting psychological scars, for he has become something of a budding amateur cook. He loves experimenting and trying new ideas and the kitchen regularly resembles a bomb site, with YouTube recipe clips playing on his tablet and utensils and food everywhere, sometimes accompanied by a strong smell of burning. He has just moved in with his girlfriend, Alice, and they host dinner parties at which Tom revels in showing off some of his gastronomic skills. Alice's parents live and work in Dubai and Tom has never met them before, but they are coming to the country for a rare visit and, before he knows it, Alice has invited them for dinner at their new flat, with Tom, naturally, being the star chef tasked with producing a gourmet three-course meal.

Meeting the in-laws for the first time is a pressure event in itself. The importance of making a good impression combined with the added pressure of cooking a showpiece meal is something few of us would welcome. Tom is understandably anxious, but if we look at his preparation for the event, we can see the first of the three aspects of my practice-management system in action.

On those occasions when Tom has had some spare time and decided to have a go at cooking a recipe or seeing if he can improve an aspect of his technique, he is doing repair. He's got a Jamie Oliver video clip playing, a cookbook with explicit instructions and, if he's making, say, a pie, he's working on his pastry-making skills. The outcome isn't important at this stage: he isn't making it for anyone but himself, there are no guests to concern himself with, and if he burns it or overworks the dough he'll just adapt and have another go.

Fundamentally, repair is working on technique. In the last chapter, we talked about your 'Feel' folder on the desktop plus your one procedural key to occupy your conscious thoughts. We said that this folder should not be opened when performing under pressure, as doing so will lead to information overload when you need it least. However, in between performing the skills under pressure, it is always a good thing to open up the folder and review the contents, making sure all the documents are present and correct. No doubt you will sometimes be making edits here and there, strengthening the content of one or two and updating others in light of recent events, before saving and closing them all for the next time you use the folder.

It's vital to keep your documents up to date, or you'll be using inadequate information for the task you're attempting. (To hark back to an earlier metaphor, the base of your iceberg will start to become weaker and more unstable.)

We talked in Chapter 3 about outcome avoidance. When someone becomes too fixated on an outcome, they tend to compromise their commitment to learning a technique thoroughly. If Tom was preoccupied with putting together the perfect three-course meal when he practised, would he be giving his all to the specific components?

It would surely be best for Tom to practise the courses separately and individually, with his recipe books to hand, as part of his repair, before doing it all together and concerning himself with the overall outcome. Of course, removing an outcome altogether simply isn't possible for Tom, as he will still have a finished plate of food even when he practises one course at a time. However, he should at least give himself the freedom to fail in his repair while he improves his technique. Tom's soufflé might sink and require him to begin again, but this is the time to do it, rather than on the big occasion.

Repair sometimes bears little comparison with the ways a technique will eventually be employed. We've mentioned rugby players kicking into a net, which would obviously never happen in a match, and I've had some strange looks from fellow coaches when I've had Jonny Wilkinson work on an aspect of his technique by deliberately kicking *under* the crossbar on the training field from close range.

It's the same when we work on our repair in everyday life. You might prepare to make a speech by delivering it in front of a mirror at home, but you obviously won't be doing this when it's for real, just as, when Tom hosts a dinner party, he won't have You-Tube clips playing and recipe books everywhere. But these methods are essential for *learning* the skill.

Training

Once Tom has reached a certain degree of competence and is able to make his pie or bake his cake without YouTube or a recipe book, he can start producing them as part of his repertoire. He might cook dinner during the week for him and Alice after a busy day at work and, over a period of time, he'll repeat the techniques he worked on in his repair as he regularly cooks the same dishes, outside of a pressured environment, no guests or decorum to worry about, just as part of a meal at home . . .

Training is basically repetition. If we imagine repair as the starting point, working on parts of the technique, and the match as the performance at the other end of the continuum, training is somewhere in the middle. We've moved on from working on a technique and we're now repeating this learned skill. Here, we become more aware of the outcome – after a busy day at work, it's undoubtedly important for Tom's cooking to be of an edible standard – and explicit coaching takes on less relevance. Small adjustments here and there – quickly checking a recipe to be sure – or a brief word of advice are fine, but training should be the repetition of something we are doing correctly and getting the desired result.

When working with professional sportspeople, getting the training aspect right can be a delicate balancing act. By the very nature of repetition, even with the utmost commitment to practice, the concentration levels of most people waver when continually repeating the same exercise. It is extremely difficult to maintain a high level of concentration throughout each repetition.

When in training mode, a player will prepare fully for his first shot; this is almost a match behaviour moment – one chance to get it right – so it merits his or her full attention. But then the second shot is executed with the knowledge and experience gleaned from the first effort just moments earlier. Despite our best intentions, it's natural for our brains to start making assumptions based on the previous experience and not prepare quite as fully as we would when we came to it cold. By the third shot, the temptation increases as the experience to draw upon has doubled. If their first shot veered a little left, they would make the adjustment to bring it right. If we return to our paper-ball throw at the start of the book, how much more confident would you be of hitting the bin if you had three shots rather than one?

Although the situation rarely occurs in match conditions, repetition is important. It is only through repeating an action that we can hope eventually to relegate it to our subconscious. So it's a trade-off: I find that players can rarely maintain anything approaching full concentration – taking dead aim – for more than five or six shots. They'll tend to hit several consecutive good ones and then, for no apparent reason, send one wildly off target. When I ask them why, they usually concede that they hadn't been concentrating fully as they'd made assumptions based on their previous shots. They'd become complacent.

I encourage repetitive training in sets of five or six maximum, with a short break to reset before starting the next set. The process of resetting improves the depth of learning, providing time to take stock and reflect, and nudges the situation closer to match behaviour – one shot, one opportunity. It's an approach someone practising a piece of music might use – a few run-throughs, a break, then start a new set as though for the first time. Rehearsing for a local am-dram production could be done in the same manner, or, indeed, training for a waste-paper bin throw.

Rather than just taking a breather, breaks could be used to practise another relevant activity: the golfer might hit a few putts so that when they come back to driving they've truly reset; the footballer could alternate penalties with long-range free-kicks; the pianist could work on command posture in front of a mirror when not playing.

This training also embodies the idea of accountability. I ask for Top Pocket scores and record the accuracy of each and every attempt. Where did the ball go? Did the outcome match the intention? Not recording outcomes turns deliberate practice into aimless practice. How else is someone to celebrate progress? The pause while I note the outcome also acts as a break between attempts, so that the next try feels closer to being the first.

A record of your training is essential if you want to progress towards your goals, whether it's to lose weight, get fit or gain muscle. Keep all the details: the machine you use; the level of difficulty; the number of reps or distance travelled; the time taken and any other pertinent information. Only through recording this information will you be able accurately to measure your progress. Many people now take their smartphones into the gym so they can listen to music, and you could easily record the information on there, or even take a piece of paper and a pencil in with you.

This allows you to create *facts*. Say you were running five kilometres on the treadmill two weeks ago and now you're running six, it is a *fact* that you are one kilometre better. If you were lifting five kilograms more on a weight machine than you were last week, it is a *fact* that you are that much stronger. Recording this produces objective data to prove you're making progress so it is a *fact* that you're getting better.

I understand how difficult it can be in our busy lives to find enough time just to make it to the gym two or three times a week, never mind having to record all this information, which probably feels a bit like 'homework', but it is the best way to make the most effective use of your precious time. Too many people go to the gym and do the same sets of cardio and weights workouts each time and wonder why they aren't moving nearer to their goals. In fact, our bodies are extremely good at adjusting to the strains we regularly place them under, and after that initial burst of benefit from your exercise regime – you get that little bit fitter or stronger – your body quickly adjusts and the effects of the same exercise plateau, as it isn't enough to take you to the next level.

In order to improve we need to adopt the no-limits mindset and continually push at the margins of our performance, which means that once you've done a week or two of the same routine, you need to start increasing either the reps or weight that you're lifting, or the distance, speed or difficulty level you're working with on the cardio equipment. Having accurate records of this information will allow you to see the improvements you make week on week and month on month, as your aimless gym routines instead become deliberate practice – worthwhile training that will maximize the use of your time in the gym and see you reach your goals much quicker. But I must emphasize that you note progress to celebrate, get excited and feel good about yourself. After all, with the amount of work, social and family pressures many of us are under, we should treat our time with the respect it deserves and that means if you spend time in the gym, you should be getting the most out of it – and enjoying it, too.

Match

By now Tom regularly rolls out the dishes he has learned through his repair and honed through his training, and, as the date of his three-course meal for the in-laws approaches, he has moved closer to match behaviour through cooking them at the dinner parties he hosts for friends. Here, he will experience conditions closer to those he can expect when the in-laws visit: the food needs to be of a good standard to appease the guests, he needs to keep the kitchen and dining area presentable and he needs to be adept at keeping the right balance between being a good chef and a good host – multitasking under pressure. Equally, this isn't *exactly* the same kind of pressure he'll experience on the big day, as he's comfortable with his friends and they're likely to be more forgiving of a blunder, but it is a significant step up from his training, which on occasion may well have ended up with him and Alice tucking into their food in front of the television after a hard day at work. Here, the other factors that will be paramount – the social aspect, the tidying up after himself as he goes, the pressure to produce that one great meal – are brought sharply into focus.

All this is excellent practice and precisely what is needed for the big day, and this final aspect of our practice is the most challenging to arrange. 'Match' is simply match behaviour, but how can we possibly replicate the difficulties someone will face on the day?

In Tom's case he was almost able to replicate match behaviour through hosting dinner parties beforehand. He may not even have been aware that he was doing it, aside from being keen to test and refine his menu, but the other factors, the cooking and hosting at the same time, would all have been invaluable practice for him. Sportspeople each have their own unique challenges to face and attempt to prepare for on match day, but 'one shot, one opportunity' should be the guiding force of this type of practice. The golfer may have prepared diligently through repair and training, but have they legislated for other factors that could affect their behaviour: the changing weather, the different tee times? A rugby goal kicker knows he will have to kick the ball throughout the game, but in a chaotic and unpredictable match he will have no idea where on the pitch he will be taking these kicks from. In short, how do we prepare for the intensity of the match?

Table 4 Match behaviour matrix

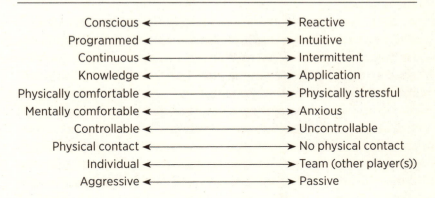

Conscious ⟷	Reactive
Programmed ⟷	Intuitive
Continuous ⟷	Intermittent
Knowledge ⟷	Application
Physically comfortable ⟷	Physically stressful
Mentally comfortable ⟷	Anxious
Controllable ⟷	Uncontrollable
Physical contact ⟷	No physical contact
Individual ⟷	Team (other player(s))
Aggressive ⟷	Passive

Perhaps the most simple point to address first is: what exactly is the match behaviour? I have developed a match behaviour matrix, the result of years of work in sport (Table 4). Whatever the activity, it can be plotted on here. Granted, physical contact isn't something for Tom to worry about when he's hosting his dinner with the in-laws – though he must be sure to get that handshake with the father right and is it one kiss on the cheek or two with the mother? However, things like anxiety, knowledge, controllable aspects can all be plotted on the matrix so that we can look at how best to replicate those match conditions in practice.

If we take two sports, let's say football and golf, and compare them on the matrix, we can begin to see the different behaviours we need to produce for the relevant activity. Golf would certainly be more programmed and football more intuitive, with little time to think. Golf, with its lengthy breaks between shots, would be intermittent, while the constant rush of a football match would be more continuous. The golfer can control more – neither can control the weather, but the golfer has a more controllable performance as it's all down to themselves, while the footballer has the uncontrollable opposition team to worry about. Golf, naturally, would lean towards the individual – with all due respect to the caddies and coaches – while football would be at the team end of the matrix.

Let's compare two activities that require a great deal of practice: acting in a local theatre production and performing a piano recital. The actor would lean towards the reactive side, as they'd need to be able to respond to the human element that is the other cast members; both would lean towards the programmed end of the spectrum, the piano player more so, given that a perfect rendition shouldn't involve doing any intuitive ad libs, while the knowledge required would be similar: they would each need to remember their lines and notes respectively, though the quick-thinking actor would have more margin for error in this respect. Both would be anxiety-inducing – stage fright would be a real risk, perhaps more so for the piano player who performs alone; physical contact might be involved for the actor, who would be closer to the team side of the matrix as part of a cast, while the piano soloist would be on the individual side.

Both have a well-tried method of recreating match behaviour: rehearsals. An actor would undoubtedly spend a lot of time on their own learning their lines (repair), and there would be various read-throughs to get used to their positions and prompts on the stage (training), but their match-behaviour practice would be the dress rehearsal. Likewise, the members of an orchestra might practise separately but rehearse together and play the full, conducted piece prior to the first performance. For the solo pianist this might be different, but a good match practice would be to run through the whole recital on the stage on which they'll be performing, with a real 'one shot, one opportunity' mentality.

Look to your own lives and see how you can apply the match behaviour matrix to your own pressure situations. If you have a presentation to make in front of a large audience, where do the various aspects sit on the matrix? How can you best use this to provide match practice before the big event? If you're going on a cycling holiday in a mountainous region of France in a couple of months with a group of cyclists a step or two up from your current ability and fitness level, how would you plot it on the matrix? You might have very little free time to spend riding, so what would you do to make your practice really count – to make it match practice?

Your Perfect Match

Trying to replicate match behaviour in practice can be complicated – because there are several different behaviours required during the activity. If we take a game like cricket, the bowler has his six balls, before he becomes a fielder for at least the next six. Fielding requires a different type of behaviour (and a range of them too: a fielder near the boundary will have a different mindset from one fielding close to the batsman; the latter is likely to have self-preservation higher in their list of priorities, as well as needing sharp reflexes, while the former may find keeping their concentration the greater challenge). As for the batting side, the striker would have a different set of priorities from the one at the other end. The wicketkeeper would require a different behaviour again, as they would face every ball bowled throughout the innings. The next to bat, waiting in the pavilion to come out, have to be always in a state of readiness.

Tom would face a similarly diverse challenge. He'd need his cooking skills, of course, but then a different set of priorities would be necessary while he was sitting down and eating – polite conversation, playing the dutiful and suitable partner for Alice, table manners and the like. All these different aspects would benefit from practising match behaviour, and it's vital that the right attitude is brought to this match practice.

When I first got involved with the England and Wales Cricket Board I was invited to watch a training session. It was fascinating, witnessing the skills of the bowlers and batsmen while they practised in the indoor nets and, at the end of the session, all the coaches gathered together to review the day.

When I was asked my opinion I initially felt uneasy – after all, I was predominantly a rugby coach at the time – so I opened by lauding the skills of the players and the efficacy of the practice activities . . . until it was clear that Kevin Shine and his fellow coaches Gordon Lord, the director of elite coaching, and Peter Moores, the then England head coach, could see right through me. 'Come on,' they said. 'It's for our benefit. What do you *really* think?'

I told them the truth: I couldn't tell when the session actually started. This was met by stony silence, so I continued, saying that if the point of the sessions was to replicate the match intensity, where players have to deliver on demand – one shot, one opportunity – I just couldn't see it. The players had drifted into the session, with the bowlers starting by more or less just turning their arms over as they warmed up and the batsmen benefiting from a similar approach as they played these easy balls to get their eye in before the pace was increased.

The silence by this time was deafening. To be clear, I wasn't faulting the commitment and skill of either the players or the coaches, all of whom I hold in very high regard, but this was hardly match practice. I continued: 'A Test match starts with a bang – the first bowler charges in to dominate and destroy the opening batsman. But he only has one first ball, so when do the players have the opportunity to rehearse the Test match behaviour?'

It was so different from rugby training sessions where, in such a hostile, contact sport, the players do their physical and mental warm-up elsewhere, so that once they cross the white line of the training pitch it's full-on match intensity – though admittedly the players more often work against pads or machines so as not to cause injury. I suggested the cricketers could do their warm-ups and preparation in a separate set of practice nets before they went into the 'business time' nets where no quarter was given: the bowler had to produce their best ball straight away, just like a Test match.

After we discussed it in some depth, the idea was adopted and to this day is still used by the performance squad. This separation of warm-up and business time in the nets helped produce a more realistic experience, putting both the batsmen and bowlers under pressure.

Game, Set and Match

Match practice is undoubtedly the most difficult facet of the three to bring to your preparation. In contact sports such as rugby, American football and Australian Rules football, there has to be a balance between reproducing the intensity of the match scenario and keeping the players free from injury. Through using the match behaviour matrix, it is possible to identify the aspects of the match scenario that you need to reproduce in your practice. What are the aspects you can identify to give you that 'one shot, one opportunity' feeling before you take to the big event itself?

For the actor discussed earlier, the demands of their match behaviour matrix were well served by the various stages of rehearsal, culminating in the full dress rehearsal which would provide them with the closest possible match behaviour. For Tom, it was, much like the multiple roles the cricketer takes on during a match, a set of different match behaviours required at different times – and sometimes all at once: cooking, hosting, keeping both himself and his home presentable. He leaned towards programmed *and* intuitive, continuous *and* intermittent, and so it was that the best way to replicate this behaviour was through a series of more informal dinner parties. This was his match practice.

If you have a difficult interview for a job coming up, then to take your preparation closer to match you could do some role play with a partner, friend or family member and get them to test you with some tricky questions. If you have a speech to deliver, whether it's for work or as part of a social engagement, then performing it with just your cue cards to refer to in front of an audience – even if it's just one person – is taking it closer to match. It's easy to feel a little silly or self-conscious when doing this, but it's quite incredible the difference doing something that little bit closer to 'for real' can make. You'll be amazed at the things you hadn't noticed before and the valuable feedback you'll receive. No matter how uncomfortable you might feel doing it now, you'll be feeling a whole lot sillier on the big day if it doesn't go to plan.

Improving performance in anything we do is a combination of the three aspects of preparation – repair, training and match. In repair we work on parts of the process and in training we repeat these parts, hardwiring the improved technique and relegating parts of it to our subconscious where necessary. All three parts of the preparation are important – one is no good without the other, just as simply doing the repair and the training will not provide the entire spectrum of experience necessary to ready ourselves fully for the event. The real challenge of all our work in repair and training is to see if it will hold up under the pressure of match conditions – before we expose ourselves to the event itself.

Principle 5: Behaviour

Skill acquisition managed as a behavioural change develops higher levels of performance under pressure.

Skill acquisition managed as a 'bolt-on' allows us too many options/choices that interfere with our ability to perform under pressure.

6.ENVIRONMENT

6.

Expecting the Unexpected

It was 0800 hours on a bright summer's day at the Royal Marines' training camp just outside Exeter. The men in combat fatigues climbed into the waiting trucks outside the officers' mess, but something wasn't quite right. Granted, the men looked fit and healthy, but they were all sorts of shapes and sizes: some were well over six foot tall and built like the proverbial brick outhouse, while others were smaller, more wiry; there was something jarring about the contrast.

Once loaded, the trucks drove off, initially heading down the main road outside the camp before turning on to a country lane and then a dirt track. After a couple of miles down the winding track, the trucks pulled up at a disused quarry, where the men disembarked. As they did so, a bit of banter started about how hard and uncomfortable the seats were – how it was nothing like flying business class.

This was the England rugby union squad preparing for the 1999 World Cup: we were a long way from our five-star hotel in Surrey. The officers addressed us and explained that we were about to be put through a series of challenges designed to test our leadership, ability to work in a team and use our initiative in environments that would be both mentally and physically challenging. The sergeant major barked out our names, dividing us into eight groups of seven or eight, and then each group was marched out to their own part of the quarry.

My group spent the morning absorbed in a series of taxing

tests. First, we had to carry four mortars plus ammunition to the top of the quarry and then assemble them so they were ready to fire. The equipment was extremely heavy and we had to work as a team to coordinate the best way to get it up the hill. Next was the dead man's slide, a 300-foot ropeline which saw us glide some fifty feet over the treeline before landing in a clearing, hearts pounding and boyhood fantasies of action heroism being fulfilled, where we then had to arrange large tyres in size order on three fence posts. The catch? We weren't allowed to touch the ground, so we had to walk on the tyres themselves and then manhandle them on to the posts.

After trudging back up the dusty rock path to the top of the quarry, our next task was to begin with us abseiling one by one down the cliff face, a good 150 feet by my reckoning. My turn came soon enough and, hooked on a line, I leaned back over the edge, my feet apart . . . and slowly let myself go. I was tentative at first, but I soon gained in confidence as I pushed away from the rock face, rappelling down quickly. What a rush!

When I reached the foot of the cliff a marine was waiting, butler-like, with a tray covered in a cloth. 'You have ten seconds to remember these items,' he said as he pulled away the cloth and started counting. With my heart still pounding and adrenaline flowing, I did my best to absorb the contents of the tray. He replaced the cloth, fastened me to a different line and signalled to the top of the cliff. 'One, two, three, GO!' he shouted.

If I'd thought going down was exciting, I hadn't experienced anything yet. On the marine's signal, three of my teammates at the top, all clipped to the same line, sprinted off down a path, hoisting me up at some speed. I practically bounced up the cliff face. At the top another marine handed me a pad and pencil and said, 'You have twenty seconds to write down everything you saw on the tray down there.' No pressure, then.

So the morning went on, with further challenges for us to navigate, as a combination of mental and physical fatigue and the pressure of having to make quick decisions in an unfamiliar environment weighed upon us. As we broke for lunch, using standard military rations and equipment, the quarry was ablaze with the flare of Primus stoves and the buzz of chatter as we all compared 'war stories'. When a whistle blew, the whole atmosphere changed.

'You all need to clear the quarry. The helicopters will pick you up in the field north of here in ten minutes. The helicopters will not wait, gentlemen.' Mild panic set in – which way was north? – as we packed up our unfinished lunches and made for the field. We scrambled out of the quarry and through bushes and trees while two Sea King helicopters thundered overhead, the trees bending in their downdraft. When we finally reached the field, the helicopters were on the ground, their blades still turning, ready to take off. We ducked down as we approached them and boarded. Where next?

The answer was a Royal Navy air station, RNAS Yeovilton. We touched down and filed out of the helicopter and into a large hangar. We changed from our combat togs into jump suits and took our seats in a classroom. 'Now,' announced the instructor, 'we are going to take you through the procedure when your helicopter has to ditch at sea.'

Thinking that this was going to be a theory session, the attention level was courteous at best, given the morning we'd all had. The gist of it was that, when a helicopter crash lands in the sea, the people on board who drown tend to be those who try to get out too early. The pressure of the water on the outside is much greater than that of the air pocket inside the helicopter, so when they force open the window or door, the pressure of the water rushing in pushes them back into the submerging cabin. The way to escape demands an incredible amount of self-discipline under the severest pressure of all: the risk of death. It is necessary to wait in the cabin while it fills with water, tilt your head back and take in large breaths of air, let the water rise, count to at least thirty – yes, thirty! – then swim through the gaps where the windows would have been.

It came as something of a surprise to learn that we'd be attempting this in an environment as close to real as possible. We were taken to a huge, deep pool, above which, suspended by a cable, was the cabin of a Lynx helicopter. 'It's about your own preparation,' the instructor said. 'When the pilot calls "ditch", check for the nearest window and put your arm on the rail towards it, as this will tell you where it is when you're underwater.'

At the side of the pool were four divers in full scuba gear carrying torches. We were divided into groups of six and my group was ordered into the helicopter cabin. I noted the railing and the nearest window. The crane lifted the cabin and the divers jumped into the pool. My heart was pounding by now, of course, in anticipation of what was to come, and, as we hung above the pool, those among the squad who couldn't swim became extremely nervous indeed. The instructor shouted through his loudhailer one last time: 'Remember to hold on. Wait for the water to rise and take a deep breath, count to thirty and follow your arm out the window.'

'*Ditch!*' The cabin dropped, thumping on to the water. We all let out involuntary gasps as we started to sink, the water coming into the cabin and starting to rise. Every man was concentrating on his own survival. As the water rose higher, I tilted my head back, took one last big breath and held it as the water covered our heads. I opened my eyes and looked at the window I needed to swim through . . . seventeen, eighteen, nineteen . . . The urge to bolt was almost overwhelming, but we held steady . . . twenty-six, twenty-seven, twenty-eight . . . The man next to me had not moved yet and I was suddenly struck by the fear that he couldn't count to thirty . . . thirty-one, thirty-two, thirty-three . . . But then he turned to swim out of the window – and I wasn't far behind. When we reached the surface we were greeted by a huge round of applause from the other groups – and an even bigger sense of relief to have made it out.

After the other groups had their turn, we were told that, in fact, when a helicopter ditches the cabin often capsizes because of the weight of the gyro on top of it. Still wet and not a little shaken from our initial dip, we were going in again. We all took the same seats in the cabin, where we at least felt confident of knowing where the nearest window was, only to be told: 'Right, change seats!' This time, I was right by the window and was certain that I at least knew how to count to thirty.

We thumped down on the water, bobbled for a second or two, then flipped over. We were now effectively sitting on the ceiling, upside down underwater and counting to thirty. My hand on the rail by the window was my only way out. When the time came, I twisted and turned a bit and eventually found my way through, followed by a couple of my teammates. This time when we surfaced the cheers were more heartfelt – it had taken us much longer. In one of the later groups, a frogman would have to rescue someone from the capsized cabin.

Finally, in our dripping, shaken condition we were dealt one last surprise: 'Many operations are carried out at night, so it is imperative that we are prepared for these conditions.' Now the torches the divers were carrying earlier made sense. In the cabin we again had to change seats – this time I was one away from the window – and then the lights went off. My eyes had barely had time to adjust to the dark when I heard the call, 'Prepare to ditch!' and down we went again.

Whoosh! We capsized once more and we were upside down in the dark trying to count to thirty. The disorientation in the dark was incredible: which way was up? I didn't have a clue where I was, but I still had hold of the rail. However, I had managed to twist myself during the crash and my shoulder felt like it was going to pop. I was still counting – twenty-eight, twenty-nine, thirty – before I somehow managed to untwist myself and head for the window. Despite a couple of good, solid kicks to the head from the guy in front, I made it to the surface. The lights went on and the cheers came again. I was shaking from all the excitement as I pulled myself out of the pool. This was not what I had been expecting when I sat down for breakfast in the officers' mess that morning.

Dislocated Expectations

Our day with the marines didn't end there. As we boarded the trucks in anticipation of heading back for a cup of tea and a restful evening, we were instead dumped in the countryside five miles from the barracks and told to find our way home on foot without being spotted from the tarmac roads. By now grumbling had started. 'What's this got to do with rugby?' muttered one. But then we realized that, with darkness encroaching, our priority had to be getting back. Plenty of people have got lost on Dartmoor and suffered from exposure.

It was an exhausted set of men who marched back into camp that night. Morale was still pretty good, with a bit of banter and singing to keep us going through our march, but we all bore the signs of those who'd had their expectations dashed one too many times: lunch unfinished as we were dragged off to the helicopters; a five-mile march instead of heading for home after feeling like we'd risked life and limb in the helicopter crash simulator.

And that, basically, was the point of the exercise: training based on dislocated expectations. Despite what the grumbling player said, dislocated expectations have absolutely everything to do with rugby – and indeed any pressure environment we enter into. While we can prepare to the best of our abilities to anticipate the behaviour required of us, and we can prepare for the environment itself, there are always going to be things we haven't predicted. So how *are* we supposed to prepare for these? The armed forces is one of the best places to look to for inspiration.

The entire philosophy of the Royal Marines' training is based on dislocated expectations. They can have the best intelligence available to them, but in a combat zone they can never be entirely sure exactly what they are going to be faced with. If a platoon climbs a cliff face and the haystack they could see from miles away turns out to be a tank, the soldiers have to deal with it and make new decisions based on an entirely different – dislocated – set of expectations.

In order to be able to improvise like this, to make effective decisions based on an always changing and unpredictable environment, the soldiers must be trained relentlessly in a similarly unpredictable manner. Our day with the marines gave us a glimpse into this: at no stage did we know what was coming next or have time to figure out how to best meet the challenge in front of us, and, through chatting with some of the marines throughout the day, we heard tales of the soldiers being woken in their bunks at 2 a.m. to go on surprise training manoeuvres, often in testing circumstances.

I had an illuminating conversation with one of the frogmen, who was a member of the Special Boat Service (SBS) – the naval equivalent of the SAS. He talked about the 'state' people get into for an operation and the difficulty involved in 'coming down' from a tour. What stayed with me most was the fact that a lot of covert operations get to the brink of execution before being called off at the last minute – far more than there were actual completed missions.

Think about that for a moment: putting in all that preparation, both mental and physical, readying yourself for a combat zone where you'd be making life-or-death decisions in unfamiliar parts of the world, the build-up of adrenaline, the taming of fear, accepting that you could be the one who pulls that trigger . . . and then being ordered to stand down at the last minute. How difficult must it be to prepare, knowing that you might not even be required to go through with it, but that any fraction of a percentage of complacency in your preparation could cost you your life, should the operation go ahead?

The equivalent might be for a bride on her wedding day to go through her pre-wedding nerves, get dressed with her friends and mother and then head to the church, pull up, take a deep breath, get out and walk towards the church doors, her brides-maids carrying the train of her dress . . . only to receive a call telling her the wedding was off today. It might be on again the next day or the day after. She'd need to be ready.

The marines' training is geared to prepare them to expect the unexpected, to produce a mindset that says, 'Whatever the oper-ation, however uncertain the circumstances, we can succeed here,' and this was what we wanted to instil in the players and staff. An international rugby match is an unpredictable, hostile environment. We can scout the opposition, watch videos of pre-vious matches and be as well prepared in terms of intelligence regarding our opponents as we like, but we can never know *exactly* what is going to happen on the field of play.

It's the same in any of our lives. The interview or test you're preparing for is a hostile environment, in which you will be pushed and tested to produce your best. You can have all the information in the world, but you can't plan for exactly which questions you'll be asked. Say you're driving in Rome for the first time. You can get all the intel you like, everything from which side of the road to drive on to the design of their road signs to making a virtual journey using Street View, but you can't plan for everything. You can't plan for the actions of other drivers or pedestrians. And, when you follow your satnav to what looks like a dead end, with a queue of angry drivers honking their horns at you from behind, it is down to you as to whether you're able to adjust to the dislocated expectations or have a meltdown behind the wheel in the hot Roman sun.

The challenge is to try to replicate the marines' approach to preparation, so that we can make effective decisions under pressure when the environment we're performing in provides circumstances we haven't – and often couldn't have – predicted. Like the marines, we wanted to produce players who could take this dislocation of expectation in their stride.

Of course, it isn't just in the marines where a constant state of readiness and an ability to meet dislocated expectations in a controlled, effective manner in what could be an environment of violent chaos is required. It's a prerequisite for those brave and committed souls working in the emergency services – for a policeman, fireman, doctor, nurse, paramedic, coastguard or ambulance driver who might suddenly have to deal with a terrible accident, a violent incident or even a terrorist attack. A nurse in an emergency department might be treating a sprained ankle one minute and a gunshot wound the next.

Dislocation is something we can all try to anticipate to ward off complacency: if we can emulate the marines and their constant state of readiness, then we can better prepare ourselves for the unforeseen moments and challenges life throws up. Our lives are nothing if not unpredictable, and while we can do our best to plan and prepare for specific pressure environments, sometimes pressure situations can come at us from nowhere: a phone call from a hospital; an impromptu call into your manager's office at work; a letter out of the blue from a creditor. We can learn much from the marines and the emergency services with their calm, methodical, level-headed decision making that is required for such taxing moments.

At the time of the camp, we, the coaching staff, had been working with most of the players for about two years and we felt we knew them pretty well. Interestingly, when we asked the marines afterwards who out of the players they thought would perform when needed and who would not, the names they gave us proved over the next couple of months to be 100 per cent correct.

At the time of the Royal Marines experience, there was a feeling among the coaches and some of the players that the squad was getting a bit too precious, becoming overly concerned with things that weren't relevant to winning a Test match. The details were starting to dictate the structure, rather than working to aid us in our overall aim. After this we started to look at things differently, with the simple overriding question: 'Would this have cost us the Test match?'

Although this camp was undertaken as preparation for the 1999 World Cup, I felt it had a lasting impact on the culture of the squad, and that this contributed to our winning the competition in 2003. The organization of the squad by this stage had become much more performance orientated, with one of Clive Woodward's great strengths being his ability to manage the political side of things himself so that the coaches could be left to do the coaching, something I valued very highly and didn't fully appreciate until he left the England team. The attitude within the group shifted from 'What are we allowed to do?' to one of 'We'll do whatever it takes to get better.'

What we really wanted the players to take away from the marines is this ability to cope with the surprises and challenges that any unpredictable situation can bring about. This is a skill in itself, to be able to manage the environment effectively when it is at odds with your expectations, and it was a skill we were desperate to instil in the players, as we'd learned a lesson the hard way some four years previously at the 1995 Rugby World Cup.

The Jonah Factor

It was June 1995 in South Africa and we'd just beaten Australia in a tense quarter-final of the Rugby World Cup. Next up was New Zealand. At that time, rugby union was still an amateur sport, so I was present, but not part of the official team because, like most of the specialists accompanying the squad, I was deemed professional. In the amateur era, the role of the head coach – it was Jack Rowell then – was to 'coach by consent', playing second fiddle to the captain, who was the man 'in charge'.

We started the week with a two-day break in Sun City to give the players some mental and physical recovery time after their exertions against Australia, so we flew from Cape Town to

Johannesburg, made the coach journey to Sun City then came back for a couple of short sessions on the Wednesday and Thursday before flying back to Cape Town on Friday for the match on Saturday. (All this would be unthinkable by today's standards of professionalism and detailed preparation.)

When Friday arrived, we returned to the Newlands Stadium in Cape Town, the venue for the game, for the traditional team run-through. The players divided into groups and began a series of passing routines that demonstrated their immaculate timing – a routine known as the Auckland Grid, which was fitting, given the nationality of our opponents. It was incredible to watch – it reminded me of the days of the formation motorbike riders of the Royal Signals in the Royal Tournament or an exhibition match by the Harlem Globetrotters – and the vibe the players were giving off was energy worth bottling. But something didn't sit right. I remember turning to Jack and murmuring, 'This is impressive, but is it really relevant?' To which Jack just gave a resigned smile and a look that seemed to say, *I agree, but this is what they like doing.*

After a while the players were so impressed with the quality of their work that the captain, Will Carling, called out, 'We're ready, Jack.' Most of the team trotted off the pitch and I stayed to work with Rob Andrew on his kicking before we too left the field, just as the New Zealand team arrived for their team run. I would have loved to have been a fly on the wall for their preparation.

I'd always wondered if there was a correlation between the degree of passion with which players sang their national anthem and successful match outcomes. England would have won easily that day if there was. Instead, twenty-year-old New Zealand winger Jonah Lomu – six foot five tall and weighing in at over eighteen stone – well and truly announced himself on the world stage, as he destroyed England almost single-handedly at times. The England players, rabbits in the headlights, simply found themselves playing in an environment that was unlike anything they had ever known.

Sometimes a performer does something so incredible that it transcends their discipline, and Lomu's feats in that match belong in this bracket. Even if you aren't a rugby fan, watching his highlights on YouTube is must-see car-crash TV. For his first try, Lomu brushed off two tackles before literally trampling over the unfortunate Mike Catt. The carnage was just beginning: Lomu would score four tries in the match and New Zealand would run out comfortable winners, 45–29, the match all but over at half-time.

Afterwards, England captain Will Carling would have to apologize for his post-match remarks in which he labelled Lomu a 'freak' – the description meant more as a compliment to his ability than anything unkind – and, to bring up car-crash TV once again, England winger Tony Underwood would go on to star alongside his nemesis in a Pizza Hut advertising campaign. (Pizza Hut made something of a theme out of using sportsmen who had failed to deliver under pressure: footballer Gareth Southgate – who missed a crucial penalty in England's Euro '96 semi-final exit to Germany – would go on to star in such an advert along with fellow penalty-missers Stuart Pearce and Chris Waddle.)

During the rugby match, England's players were shell-shocked. A player of Lomu's size should not have been able to run that fast, should he? And he certainly shouldn't have been playing on the wing – a position for fast, slight-of-build players, surely? How were they expected to tackle him when his legs were the size of a normal person's body?

But let's take another look at this, through the prism not only of England's inability to react to their dislocated expectations, but also of their failure to prepare fully for the environment. During the week there had been an eighteen-stone, lightning-quick elephant in the room. Other than a single mention during a team meeting, the New Zealander barely even warranted comment. There was no strategy put in place to account for a player with such unique talents, no practice devised to help the likes of poor Tony Underwood cope with him – and he certainly wasn't alone in needing this practice. Underwood was unable to do anything that would even begin to replicate the environment he would face on match day.

Now, Jonah Lomu was a phenomenon at the peak of his powers, but could England have done anything differently? Lomu was not a kept secret. He didn't explode from nowhere to devour England; he had played for New Zealand in the seven-a-side team prior to the World Cup, and indeed had starred throughout the tournament, notably against Ireland and later, in the quarter-final, Scotland, scoring tries that demonstrated his strength and speed. In short, the intel was there, but England chose not to act on it, instead preferring to adhere to the popular sports cliché of 'concentrating on their own game rather than worrying about the opposition'. If Jack Rowell, rather than the players, had had complete control, would the situation have been different? I think so.

From a coach's perspective, we could have had the players who would be facing up to him – Underwood and the rest of the backs – practise by having the biggest players in the squad running at them. Lomu's legs were so big that the traditional method of going low when tackling was ineffective; his power was such that he simply ran through the arms of the tackler. But studying his previous matches would show that he 'hands off' opposing players, using his outstretched, non-ball carrying hand to brush them aside, so would grabbing his arm – a tactic used later by the diminutive and comparatively slight Australian George Gregan – and slowing him down this way so that other players could join in and topple the giant not have been a valid option?

The England match was arguably Lomu's greatest ever game. In both the final that followed and the subsequent Tri Nations, he didn't have quite the same dramatic impact. The reason? Other teams had noted his strengths and prepared fully to cope with him. There was no chance of any dislocation in their expectations.

This is the opposite case to the perils of using too much information described in Chapter 4. Here, ignoring relevant information proved to be a recipe for disaster, and is a mistake it is hard to imagine the Royal Marines making. The marines manage to marry the ability to respond to dislocated expectations with thorough preparation for their match environment. If the marines knew in advance that what looked like a haystack was, in fact, a tank, do you think they would wait until it started firing at them before they took action? Or would they use the intelligence to their advantage?

If we look at another, perhaps even more famous Jonah, the one who features in the Bible, we again see an example of a man who did not prepare for the opponent he was about to face: in this case, God. The biblical Jonah was swallowed by a whale, while for England, New Zealand's Jonah *was* the whale: huge, dangerous – and hiding in plain sight because they chose not to prepare properly.*

The Interview

Emily is a young magazine journalist interviewing for her second job, having accrued a good deal of experience in her role at a small, independent publication before hitting a glass ceiling. She's talented and ambitious and the role she's interviewing for is with an industry-leading magazine whose editor-in-chief is famed as a maverick genius – and, as is often the case, something of a tyrant.

Before her first interview she was told that it would be with two of the magazine's deputy editors and she prepared accordingly – researching the company history and latest publications, checking on the background of the people interviewing her, visualizing the interview environment and trying to prepare

* It was with great sadness that I learned Jonah Lomu had passed away during the writing of this book, in November 2015. He was a truly humble man who took rugby to a new level on the world sporting stage.

for any curve balls that might be thrown her way – with great success, as she achieved her goal, the second interview.

Now she's sitting in the reception area, waiting for the same people who interviewed her the first time. She's nervous but excited – her butterflies feel mobilized – and she's quietly confident. She did some follow-up research for this interview, mainly just going through her notes from the first one, and she feels good and ready. The deputy editors come out to greet her, looking a little frazzled with the magazine's deadline day looming, and they take her to the same interview room as last time . . . only to find it's occupied.

'Sorry, we really should have booked a meeting room – let's try down here,' one of them says. Emily is all smiles, unflappable. But they walk down the hall, try several more, and now the deputies seem a little concerned. 'Er, sorry about this . . .' one of them starts, until the infamous editor-in-chief walks past, ascertains the problem and, within moments, fixes it.

'Let's do it in my office,' she says. 'It would be useful for me to sit in on it anyway.'

So now the environment has suddenly shifted from the traditional sitting-across-the-meeting-table format of the first interview, to a new location with an additional participant. Emily is invited to take a seat on a suitably fashionable low-slung sofa, which is so low that she feels like she's practically on the floor; the two deputies sit together on a similar sofa opposite and the editor-in-chief looms over all, her seat a couple of feet higher, as she wheels across in her state-of-the-art office chair. Emily can't sit back in her sofa as she'd be practically horizontal, but sitting up isn't exactly comfortable either: with no back support and her bum only a couple of inches from the floor, it's like she's squatting.

What soon also becomes clear is that the editor-in-chief isn't 'sitting in' – she's running this show. She starts bombarding Emily with questions – many of which are the same as those from the first interview, but because she has already answered these questions to the deputy editors she becomes self-conscious, changing her perfectly good original answers to appease the two who've heard it all before. And the dynamic has shifted markedly: while in her first interview she had the full attention of the deputy editors, now they seem more concerned with pleasing the editor-in-chief than with interviewing her – almost like they're being interviewed too.

Emily is struggling to adapt, with the editor-in-chief, an imposing figure at the best of times, growing in stature by the second, taking on cartoonish proportions from her elevated position. Emily is starting to feel that the interview is getting away from her. Then it gets worse.

The editor-in-chief starts talking about her own history in magazine publishing, the stories she broke some ten, twenty years ago. She asks Emily her opinion on them . . . and Emily looks on, blankly. She hadn't prepared for this: she didn't do her research on the editor-in-chief. She had a certain amount of industry knowledge to fall back on, mainly information from her own brief time in magazines, but no specifics, not like she's hearing now. Emily is feeling hot and bothered and now she's panicking – this is not going well and all she wants is to get out of here with what little dignity she has left. At the end she gathers her things and leaves. She does not get the job.

Emily, like the England rugby team, was not prepared for the dislocated expectations she encountered. She met her own Jonah Lomu in the shape of the imposing editor-in-chief and she couldn't cope with it. What could Emily have done differently? Well, turning up to an interview, even if you know it's with two lieutenants, without doing your homework on the chief is what some would call a rookie mistake. She could also have spoken up and said she'd prefer to change seats. This takes confidence and, again, an ability to react promptly to dislocated expectations, but if the marines weren't happy with their position in a combat zone, they'd change it. She also allowed her self-consciousness and the altered dynamic between the three interviewers to get the better of her, when she should have had faith in her original answers.

In pressure situations, when our perception narrows and our

adrenaline is pumping, it is always best to tackle the biggest and most immediate threat in our environment. In Emily's case it was the editor-in-chief and, given that she would have been the ultimate decision maker in any hiring and firing, she should have concentrated solely on impressing her, rather than being reluctant to repeat information in front of the two deputies.

Perhaps it's too harsh to chastise Emily. She is young and relatively inexperienced, after all, just as the England rugby team were amateurs at the time they faced their own nemesis. What she must do is learn from the experience: use the intel at her disposal more effectively in future and be prepared to expect the unexpected. But how exactly can she, and we, do this?

Match Environment

Inspired by the marines' approach to preparation – the continual reviewing of their training and selection processes, the use of intelligence to inform their preparations, their readiness and ability to perform when the environment is at odds with their expectations – I have devised a match environment matrix, along similar lines to the match behaviour matrix on page 157.

Some of the entries also feature on the match behaviour matrix. Clearly there is some overlap between environment and behaviour, with the former having a strong impact on the latter. Simply put, behaviour is how someone responds when placed in a certain environment, and clearly the two overlap when it comes to preparing for a pressure event. That is why often the best way to prepare for the match behaviour is to recreate the match environment as closely as possible.

In some cases this environment is quite literally recreated. The team run in the stadium the day before a big game is a sacred rugby tradition. This is their match environment preparation, getting the players used to the environment in which they'll be performing. And it's a very valid aspect of preparation: orchestras

Table 5 Match environment matrix

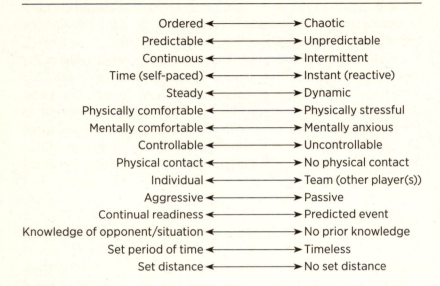

Ordered	Chaotic
Predictable	Unpredictable
Continuous	Intermittent
Time (self-paced)	Instant (reactive)
Steady	Dynamic
Physically comfortable	Physically stressful
Mentally comfortable	Mentally anxious
Controllable	Uncontrollable
Physical contact	No physical contact
Individual	Team (other player(s))
Aggressive	Passive
Continual readiness	Predicted event
Knowledge of opponent/situation	No prior knowledge
Set period of time	Timeless
Set distance	No set distance

have a run-through in the match environment before the big event, as do actors at a dress rehearsal. What's missing is, of course, the crowd, and the added pressure it can bring.

What you do in this environment counts just as much as *where* you're doing it. Those in the performing arts are better off in this respect: musicians can play their set from start to finish; actors can play their roles as if for real, a 'one shot, one opportunity' mentality. A sporting contest has to be plotted more towards the dynamic, chaotic and unpredictable side of the matrix in comparison. There is no script or score to follow, only skills to perfect. But a slick passing routine such as the Auckland Grid is hardly relevant preparation for stopping a speeding juggernaut like Lomu.

Effective opposition is vital. Consider the most public operation ever conducted by the SAS: the Iranian embassy siege in 1980, which culminated in the SAS storming the embassy, killing five of the six terrorists and rescuing twenty-three hostages.

Unusually, much of the external action was broadcast live on TV by news crews. While sports performers expect to be performing in front of an audience, it was certainly a unique factor for the SAS to have to consider.

The SAS prepared, just like the orchestra or the actors or the sports team, by trying to recreate the environment in which they were to perform. Blueprints were studied, people with first-hand knowledge of the building consulted, details about the people in the building were obtained and a mock-up of the environment was constructed for them in which to practise clearing hostages from smoke-filled rooms. The difference between the SAS and the rugby team is that they had created the environment they would be working in, one that featured a hostile opposition, whereas the rugby team, although in the literal environment, barely touched on the conditions they would face come match day. And that wasn't the only difference. Despite all their meticulous planning, things still went wrong for the SAS during their operation – a soldier accidentally broke a window, which alerted the terrorists; a fire started in the building – but they still prevailed because they were mentally prepared by their training to react accordingly. Fittingly for this particular operational environment, they didn't allow themselves to be a hostage to their plan.

If we return to Emily and her interview, how could the matrix have helped her? We would say that, in ordinary circumstances, it would not be unreasonable for her to expect to at least be physically comfortable, but as we saw, she was in an uncomfortable position – practically squatting on a low-slung sofa with the editor-in-chief looming over her – which then had significant mental repercussions. In an interview we can expect things to be mentally taxing; it can be a stressful experience with no little pressure to perform. Emily's mindset would be towards the anxiety side of the spectrum while she was preparing. But it is in the last few entries that the matrix might have best helped Emily, particularly in her 'knowledge of opponent/situation', the area where the rugby team also fell short. Emily could have done her homework on the editor-in-chief instead of just rereading her original notes and expecting the second interview to replicate the first. Continual readiness is a prerequisite of the interview experience, as an interview can be a chaotic event: the interviewee has little to no control over the script and therefore, like the rugby match, there aren't always specific lines to rehearse. The interview is largely reactive, but interviewees must also be proactive in their approach, asking questions and displaying an interest in the company.

Emily will learn massively from her experience and, as her career progresses, each interview she attends will be the ultimate kind of match practice that will eventually prove successful. And even if she had done her research more effectively, short of raiding the magazine's offices on a special-forces style reconnaissance mission, she could hardly have prepared for every eventuality.

The matrix is effectively the conditions we can plan for, because we can't predict every aspect of every environment. Sometimes, even the best-laid plan will be thrown off course by dislocation, but being prepared for it is a skill in itself, and one that is usually only mastered from experience. In short, the only way to become used to dislocated expectations can be to have them dislocated a lot. The good – or perhaps not so good – news is that life will throw up plenty of opportunities to gain this experience.

Importing Knowledge

So far we have talked about preparing for the environment in which we're to perform under pressure, but one thing this chapter – and indeed the aspects of the Pressure Principle so far discussed – should have made clear is that we can learn a great deal in our efforts to perform better under pressure by looking at the environments other people perform in. We've talked about the armed forces' approach to pressure environments, and previously we've looked at examples ranging from skateboarders to dolphin trainers as well as in my own sports specialities, and I hope you have been able to translate this to your own match environment.

Much as we should treat preparation for dislocated expectations as a skill to be learned, we should likewise learn from the knowledge and techniques other people use in their own environments – in effect, to 'import' knowledge from other fields.

Henry Ford is famous for building the 'motor car for the multitude', thanks in no small part to the productive moving assembly line he pioneered. But Ford was inspired by another environment – the production lines in Chicago meat-packing plants – and history is littered with industries taking ideas from others. Businesses do it today, regularly importing people from different areas to give an outsider's outlook. Sometimes these work, sometimes they don't.

I don't mean we should take 'big' ideas from industry into our own lives; rather, I'm talking about looking at your friends, family and colleagues and having an open enough mind to see whether you can 'import' any knowledge from the pressure environments in which they perform. Do you have a friend who has to work to a deadline, or who balances career and parenthood or finds time every morning to fit in an hour's cycling as well as holding down two jobs? How do they manage their commitments? If you are able to keep an open mind, there is no doubt much to learn from those around you.

It might just be a little tip or technique you pick up. 'No screens for an hour before bedtime,' your friend might say about switching off at night. Perhaps doing the same yourself will give you a better night's sleep and deliver a little gain when dealing with your own pressures.

I've often looked at sports other than those I coach in order to improve my knowledge and help give my own clients an advantage. I once coached a young winger from Northampton who struggled with his catching when the opposition kicked the ball high in the air towards him. I had spent some time in Australia studying the coaching of Australian Rules football and I got the lad and his fellow backs together to show them a video of the incredible overhead catches made in the Aussie game.

The players' immediate response was one of disbelief that these Australian players could launch themselves towards a high ball with their shin on another player's shoulder. But this is a bit like watching a 'goal of the month' compilation and assuming that every goal in football is a work of art. I then showed them a video of some of the practice sessions, with all the dropped catches and missed jumps as the players worked on their repair. Once they realized they didn't have to get it right first time, the rugby players were more willing to give it a go.

One of the coaching staff put a large pad on his back like a turtle shell and the players would jump up and balance for a split second on one knee on the pad to catch the ball. The results were, inevitably, amusing to watch to start with, as players fell off, mistimed their jumps and sometimes missed the ball completely – all good repair – and none were laughing more than the players themselves. Suddenly, within the comical chaos, one player got it right, taking the catch perfectly, and, after much applause, the rest soon followed. That was the start of the process, and by the time the World Cup came around in 2003, thanks in no little part to his commitment to continually improving, that winger from Northampton had become one of the strongest overhead catchers in the game.

With the support from head coach Clive Woodward, I was able to introduce a process from Australian Rules to help turn a weakness into a strength. It is wise to continually keep an open mind and explore in other environments what we can learn to help ourselves.

Environmentally Friendly

What made all this possible was the more general environment, outside the specific match environment. I was working in a culture in which, under Woodward, anything we could try or introduce to improve performance on the field was welcomed. It was a culture that, unlike many organizations trapped in a cycle of repeating what they've always done without question, encouraged change and new ways of doing things. We weren't afraid of failure in our approach – we would just try something else if it didn't work and the players, as demonstrated by their good humour when they bounced off the pads while they tried and failed and tried again, were free to bring a childlike approach to their learning.

We also drew up a series of 'teamship rules' which addressed things like how people would like to be told if they're selected for the team or not, how they should react when informed – particularly in regard to their behaviour towards their rival(s) for that spot – and common courtesy, such as agreeing to reply to texts or emails within twenty-four hours.

Selection can be an area in which environment is particularly important, and there are plenty of stories about footballers finding out they've been dropped from a squad via text, or managers discovering they've been fired on social media before they've even received the phone call. Anyone who has worked for a company in which redundancies are being made can probably empathize. Learning your fate is never pleasant, but it can be done in a sensitive and considerate style in the right environment.

Perhaps you're lucky enough to work in a culture where importing new ideas is encouraged. Or you're lucky enough to have a home environment that allows you to address the pressures you feel. As shown earlier, learning is achieved most effectively in an environment of strong encouragement, of celebrating success and with no fear or stigma attached to the idea of failure. Such moral support is vital if we are to produce our best in the match environment, and it is something most of us instinctively try to provide for our children so that they can deliver their best and effectively deal with pressure as they grow into adults.

It is useful to make this distinction because there are several different environments surrounding the event that we often need to navigate to produce our best. The marines have their practice environment and the combat environment, just as the rugby team did. Even Emily would have had her practice environment, whether that was sitting reading through her notes, going through the interview in her head or even doing a bit of role-play to prepare for the match-day environment of the interview itself.

To be most effective, practice environments should mimic the match as closely as possible. The marines used intel and preparation for the dislocation of their expectations to achieve this, but both Emily and the 1995 England rugby team failed to use their intel wisely. They weren't prepared for the dislocation in their expectations and they suffered for it.

Principle 6: Environment

Failure to deliver training and preparation in the match environment will often result in a reduced ability to perform under pressure in match conditions.

7.SENSORY SHUTDOWN

7.

Flying Your Plane

It was a warm spring day in 2006 when I walked across the tarmac at Yeovilton. *Perfect conditions*, I thought as I climbed the steps and clambered into the cockpit of the Hawk fighter jet. A technician strapped me in, plugging the radio wires from my helmet into the sockets and, finally, connecting the air hose to the nozzle on my right side.

The pilot, New Zealander Craig Complain, who was seated in front of me – all I could see was the top of his helmet beyond my instrument panel – raised his hand and made the 'thumbs up' sign. I strapped the microphone to my throat and he asked over the intercom, 'All OK back there?'

'Yup, all fine,' I said. And then the engines began to whine like a giant turbine.

I'd spent the previous four days as a guest of the Fleet Air Arm – the branch of the Royal Navy responsible for its aircraft – where I'd used simulators, been up in a Lynx helicopter and watched a training exercise in a simulator where a pilot and navigator investigated a suspicious trawler in the North Sea. The day before my flight I'd had a medical and been fitted with a flight suit, helmet, fireproof T-shirt, leggings and gloves, all ready for my *Top Gun* moment.

Now, with the engines whirring and the growing feeling that no amount of simulators can truly prepare anyone for *this*, we began to taxi down the runway. Craig talked me through the controls once again, which I was grateful for, despite learning them in the simulator the day before, because now it was real. Then he hit me with a surprise that the simulator hadn't prepared me for: 'There is a button on your right-hand side, next to your thigh, with yellow-and-black stripes.'

'Yes, found it,' I said. It was labelled EJECT.

'Good,' Craig continued. 'There's a pin on a chain just under the button. Pull it out and drop it in the hole next to the button. I will not use the word "eject" again unless I want you to hit the button. Understood?'

I understood all right. The jet rocked to a gentle halt and then the message came from ground control that we were cleared to take off. The engine's whine increased, doubling the noise it had made earlier, and we started to roll down the runway, bumping over the joints in the concrete, before there was a sudden burst of acceleration and we were airborne. And then . . . *whoosh*.

We burst forward at a speed I'd never felt before, my hands balling into fists, my knuckles white. It was as though we'd been fired from a cannon as we climbed up into the blue sky. Once we levelled out and Craig had checked I was still breathing, he said he was going to show me a few moves.

The first was a loop. As we climbed I could feel my G-suit slowly squeezing my legs, and as the turn became tighter the squeeze was rising, getting tighter and higher up my thighs and into my stomach. It felt as if my insides were being completely rearranged. This was 5G.

Craig said he was going to give me a little G-force demonstration (I thought he already had) and he put the jet into a tight turn and asked me to take my hand off the controls and put it on my thigh, which I did. Then we turned tightly again and he asked me to put it back on the controls. I could not believe what I was feeling: I was hardly able to lift my arm off my thigh – it weighed a ton. At the same time, it was like my stomach was being squeezed up into my ribcage by the G-suit.

When we levelled out he offered me the chance of a lifetime:

to take the controls myself. I gladly accepted this irresistible cocktail of power, speed, control and excitement. It was like flying a super-fast airborne go-kart – and it was just as bumpy a ride as it is on the dodgems at the fairground. It was an exhilarating experience of freedom, though my wings were clipped all too soon as Craig took the controls back.

Craig took us down to sea level, low enough to avoid radar detection. We then turned inland and constantly adjusted altitude with the lie of the land. Craig turned the Hawk on its side and I realized just how fast we were going: hedgerows, footpaths and sheep shot past in a barely registered blur.

When we finally headed for home, I had time to collect my thoughts. Craig had hardly stopped talking throughout the whole flight, commentating on what we were about to do even when we were in some of the more acrobatic manoeuvres. But that wasn't what was so impressive: it was his tone and matter-of-fact manner. He was under the same pressures of the G-force as I was, but while I was convinced my insides had been put in a cocktail shaker, Craig's voice would have suggested we were simply having a chat over coffee.

When we'd touched down and were taxiing back to the parking area, I gratefully placed the pin back in the ejector switch at Craig's request. The ground technicians freed me from my various umbilical cords to the cockpit and as I set foot on terra firma once again, my legs hardly seemed to know where the ground was, my abdominals couldn't have felt more strained if I'd done a thousand sit-ups, my shoulders were sore and my stomach ached from the inside out.

Shutting Down

How do people like Craig, who start out just like the rest of us, become so capable under pressure in an environment where a mistake could mean death? The answer lies in their ability to delay the impact of sensory shutdown.

When the pressure we are under increases, it is natural for our awareness to decrease. This change might be almost impercept- ible at first, but as the pressure increases, our peripheral vision narrows and so to does our hearing, and, as a result, so does what we are thinking. When the pressure really racks up we are virtu- ally shutting down and our awareness has narrowed to a tiny window. Now, this is a great help to us when we are in imminent danger, with our body diverting all its resources to dealing with this one problem – run for your life, get out the way of that oncoming vehicle – but it inhibits us when performing in the instances when we are *perceiving* a threat.

For the pilots, their training involves a great deal of work on delaying the impact of sensory shutdown, so that they can behave more efficiently in their highly stressful environments. As Craig demonstrated in the cockpit, a trained fighter pilot is able to maintain a higher level of awareness under pressure than a civilian. (That isn't to say it doesn't drop to some degree – just not as much as it did for the likes of me.) There are three key elements required to achieve this: awareness of the environ- ment; decision-making skills, often in an unpredictable and hostile situation and accompanied by a dislocation of expect- ation; and the functional skills of flying and navigating the plane.

After working with the training officers, I produced the Pilot Sensory Shutdown model (Figure 3), based on the sequence the pilot trainers explained to me. Every pilot goes through a sequence: fly, navigate, communicate, administrate. Which is to say: fly the plane; navigate using the horizon as well as the instru- ments; communicate with control centre and other aircraft; and administrate through checking the instruments for the status of the aircraft. I'd noticed during our flight that Craig had con- stantly been moving his head and this was because he was continually repeating the sequence.

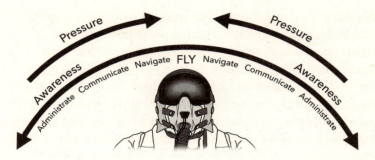

Figure 3 *Pilot Sensory Shutdown Model*

When a trainee pilot is working in the simulators and the pressure increases, the first thing to drop out of the sequence is administration. It's the least immediately vital element, and as we begin to feel the effects of pressure we're programmed to hone in on the most task-relevant aspects of a process. As pressure increases on the trainee, communication is the next to suffer, then navigation – so that, finally, the only thing the trainee is concerned about is flying the plane. The last stage is one in which the plane is flying the pilot, rather than the other way round.

So how does the trainee improve awareness and effectiveness under pressure? Firstly, it's a question of familiarity with pressure, which is why so much time is spent in the simulators dislocating expectations. The only way to get used to the pressure of dislocated expectations is to continually be in an unpredictable environment.

I sat in on one such training operation in which, soon after take-off, the location of a trawler the crew had to investigate was suddenly changed, which meant that all their original planning and flight paths had to be discarded. Then the weather in the simulator changed from the predicted clear skies to low cloud and rain, meaning that the trainees had to fly much lower.

These changes in expectation aren't just random. They are

deliberately targeted to increase pressure while testing awareness. Other dislocations might include an engine malfunction, which should be quickly noticed if the 'administrate' part of the sequence is being performed diligently.

The training officers created situations far more testing than those likely to be encountered in a real operation, at least in terms of pressure to make decisions and the degree of dislocation. This echoes Chapter 1, where we saw that going beyond where we need to be – beyond where it feels comfortable – helps get us closer to the J side of the C to J continuum, so that when it comes to performing for real, we're ready and comfortable with the adjustments required of us. This is match practice that goes beyond the intensity of the match itself.

The concept of sensory shutdown isn't limited to pilots. We see its effects when we watch sports stars perform in big events and we feel it in our own lives when we are under pressure. If you are suddenly given a major project at work with a challenging deadline – a dislocation of your expectations when you started the day – what in your own sequence is the first to suffer? It's probably your admin, just like the pilot, as that is put to one side to concentrate on the most important thing in your environment. Your communication would likely suffer too, with less opportunity to check your email or retrieve messages, perhaps missing regular briefings too – all part of your own personal sequencing. Last to go would be your navigation, the coordinates of your routine, as you were forced to cancel social engagements, stop exercising and let your day-to-day work drift to get the big job done. Now you're just flying the plane – or rather the plane is flying you.

We'll return to this idea shortly, but in the meantime let's look at an aspect of sensory shutdown we all have to deal with when performing in a pressure situation: making a decision when the adrenaline is flowing and your heart is pounding.

The Combat Zone

My experience with Craig showed me just how fit you have to be to fly a fighter jet: my body felt like it had been through a pretty intense workout. Craig told me that he did a lot of his own fitness and stability work and I knew he was a keen rugby player. He admitted that, even in his excellent physical condition, he would find three flights a day very tough on his body, even though it's a job that can be done sitting down. Formula 1 drivers have much the same problem. It's easy to think, *Well, they just drive round a circuit. Why do you need to be fit for that?* In fact, motor racing at that level is hugely demanding physically, with similarly extreme forces exerted on the driver's body. A high level of fitness is required to perform and function well.

Figure 4 demonstrates how decision-making capability and the ability to execute skills effectively reduce as heart rate (HR) in beats per minute (bpm) increases.

A healthy person's heart rate is a good indication of general level of fitness, because the fitter someone is, the lower their resting heart rate is and the longer it takes them to reach their maximum heart rate. As Figure 4 shows, this is crucial when it comes to making decisions and performing under pressure. A fighter pilot's heart rate needs to stay as close to the optimal zone as possible, because the higher it gets, the worse the ability to make decisions becomes.

Even when the heart rate gets into three figures, fine motor skills – hand–eye coordination etc. – begin to deteriorate. Think about what that would mean for a surgeon manipulating instruments in a delicate operation, or for a marine whose finger was poised over a hair trigger. The benefits of having a lower resting heart rate to begin with, achieved through a good standard of fitness, are obvious here.

There are, however, possible ways to control your heart rate. Before any tricky procedure, slowing your breathing to get some

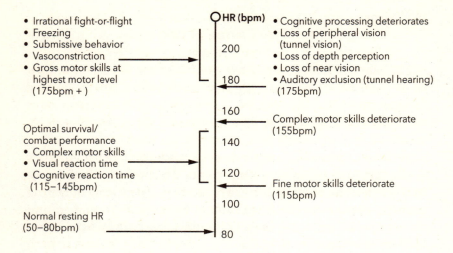

Figure 4 *Sensory shutdown under pressure*

Source: Steve Drzewiecki, 'Survival Stress in Law Enforcement', Traverse City Police Department School of Police Staff and Command Program, 2002.

oxygen in and reduce your heart rate will help you to execute the skill better. It's an approach I'd recommend to anyone, whether you're about to play a tough shot on the pool table in the local pub or preparing to walk into a room full of strangers on your first day in a job: slow your world down with some deep breaths and slower exhalations.

A heart rate of 115 to 145 bpm puts you in the combat-performance zone. This is where football and rugby players spend most of their time operating. While the fine motor skills are suffering, complex motor skills – the coordination of muscle groups to perform a series of movements at the right time – are at their peak here. For the footballer this might be dribbling, shooting or passing while running; for the rugby player it might be handing off or passing the ball while dodging tackles and running. The body is in its most effective state for these skills, as the visual and cognitive reaction time is good, so that the player can pick out a teammate with a pass, avoid an opposition player and have a good sense of the relative geography of the pitch – where the goal and touchlines are. Footballers and rugby players are 'in the game' here and feel pretty comfortable. Their high levels of fitness allow them to operate in this zone for prolonged periods, while for most of us our heart rates would be off the scale after a few minutes of frenetic high-level sport.

However, once the heart rate gets above 155, these complex skills start to deteriorate. If you've ever watched a footballer run half the length of the pitch with the ball at his feet, powering past the opposition, with teammates either side unmarked and in great positions to receive a pass, and instead he mishits a shot at goal, sending it ballooning into the stands, you might have thought, *What on earth happened there?*

The answer might well be sensory shutdown. As the player runs flat out, the increased physical exertion raises his heart rate, which in turn causes his complex motor skills to decrease, which would be a factor in his poor shot. When the heart rate gets up to around 175 the impact of sensory shutdown affects his awareness, with the peripheral vision and hearing decreasing. The player with the ball might well have been completely unaware of his teammates: in that state he couldn't see or hear them as well as he would have done had his heart rate been much lower.

In extreme conditions of mental and physical stress, where the heart rate gets above the 175 mark, fight-or-flight mode can enter the equation. This area is good if we have to run flat out or defend ourselves. It is in this region of almost blind intensity where we are on the edge of completely losing control. This is where people can feel the 'red mist' descend, which, so long as we remain on the verge of it, can be useful in a particularly aggressive sport such as boxing. But it can be a pretty unedifying sight on the rugby or football field when punches are being thrown. This tends to happen after a late tackle, when the player gets up and launches into an irrational and violent reaction. This rarely helps a team: usually the player will end up being sent off.

You will undoubtedly have experienced your own 'red mist'. When we're under pressure and absorbed in dealing with the source of it, with our heart rate raised and our awareness narrowing, it's all too easy to snap at our colleagues, friends, partners or even children who interrupt us. Once we've reached this stage, our decision-making skills have deserted us, as most of us would realize that, just like the footballer getting an early bath, there's little point getting angry at other people – particularly when they're on our side.

Match Fit

The importance of physical fitness, then, cannot be understated. Fitter people, with lower resting heart rates, take longer to get into the zone that adversely affects the task they're attempting. They are capable of making better decisions under fatigue and pressure, a vital skill in occupations such as the armed forces and the emergency services.

Consider two armed police officers chasing a suspect, one fit, the other not. They eventually corner their quarry and draw their weapons. The fitter, 'match fit' officer's heart will be beating less fast, further from sensory shutdown and allowing fine motor skills to operate more effectively. That officer would be in a better position to make a correct decision about whether to open fire than his or her less-fit colleague, whose heart rate might already have crossed the 175 barrier into red mist territory, where a rash decision could result in lives lost and ruined that might otherwise have been spared.

We might not be called upon to make life-or-death decisions ourselves, but fitness is still important. Doctors preach the importance of exercise as a stress buster, and we're all familiar with the concept of using physical exertion to let off steam, whether it's storming off for a brisk walk around the block or letting it all out on the punch bags in the gym. Lowering your resting heart rate through a regular structured exercise routine not only helps in these individual moments of stress, but also more generally it keeps us in a constant state of readiness, just like the marines, to deal with high-pressure situations.

Exercise is also said to be good for mood improvement and boosting self-esteem, which shouldn't come as too much of a surprise, bearing in mind our discussion about the body's power to inform the mind and vice versa. Feeling good about ourselves can be an invaluable aid to combating stress.

Command Posture (Again)

While we're talking about the body informing the mind, it's useful to reiterate the importance of posture. When we're under pressure we tend to become hunched – think back to the people in the traffic jam, leaning over their steering wheels, honking their horns. Sensory shutdown makes us less aware of what we're doing. So, when you're stressed and your posture is hunched and your body language poor, you probably don't even realize it.

Adopting command posture, making yourself bigger, will have a number of benefits. Firstly, as you're *consciously* adopting the posture, it will heighten your awareness of what you are doing and so combat the effects of sensory shutdown. And this posture, with your feet rooted to the ground, keeping yourself upright, will give you a stronger *feeling* of control, instead of your environment being in control of you, so that you feel more confident and positive about the challenge you're facing. It's no coincidence that Craig and I were strapped in to the Hawk in command posture, the best position in which to heighten our awareness and to be able to scan our environment. A person who is hunched and stooped forward because of pressure is looking up to a problem. A person who stands tall, in command, can look down on a challenge.

Match Commentary

Trainee pilots practising in the simulator say the sequence, 'Fly, navigate, communicate, administrate,' aloud, over and over again until it becomes ingrained. This is their simple conscious process key, their cue card to tap into the processes they need to implement. In this respect it's similar to the 'Mirror, signal, manoeuvre' self-talk used when learning to drive. To start with, we might say the key aloud, but then it will be something we say in our head and eventually it will be something we simply do implicitly. And it's the same for the pilot: by the time they're experienced and flying for real, they won't be using self-talk; they will just be *doing* it. Fly, navigate, communicate, administrate will have become a learned behaviour.

Self-talk can be an extremely useful aid to development. Trainee pilots' voices are recorded in the simulators and analysed not just for what is said but also how it's said. The trainers can gauge vocal stress, particularly any changes in response to unexpected situations – dislocated expectations. Also, knowing that they are being recorded creates a useful kind of self-consciousness in the trainee, because they need to *show* that they're in control. Being forced to show control in your voice – much like showing confidence in your body language – makes you *feel* more in control, a kind of self-fulfilling expectation.

Such real-time commentary can boost concentration and create a sense that time has slowed, enabling the next event to be anticipated rather than simply reacted to. This is a useful tip in an activity like driving, where it's easy to become complacent practising an implicit skill. Commentating on what you're doing as it happens can give a sense of focus that might otherwise be lacking, provided you aren't dredging up too much unnecessary detail. So verbally noting the things you're consciously doing – 'Turning left here . . . traffic slowing down ahead' – can anchor your thoughts in your deliberate actions and keep you focused. Commentary while driving is used in the emergency services, both in training and when the sirens are on and they are responding to an incident at speed.

But back to 'Fly, navigate, communicate, administrate'. To a pilot suffering the effects of sensory shutdown, particularly when they're relatively inexperienced, this commentary can provide a welcome way to anchor their thoughts and remind them what they need to be doing, just as a newly qualified driver experiencing stress when driving on a busy motorway for the first time might use 'Mirror, signal, manoeuvre' self-talk to regain focus.

Scanning Sequence

When we're in a pressure situation, which raises our heart rate and releases adrenaline, our peripheral vision begins to narrow. As we get higher up the heart-rate chart, so our peripheral vision narrows accordingly. Here, the scanning sequence for the pilot becomes vital. Remember that Craig's head was moving constantly throughout our flight; with his eyes seeing less, it was the continual movement of his head that allowed him to keep a good level of awareness while he repeated his internal 'Fly, navigate, communicate, administrate' sequence.

Recall from Chapter 2 the 'Crossbar, touchlines, crossbar' self-talk, which gave rugby players a greater awareness of the dimensions and spaces of the pitch. Scanning sequences like this are easy-to-remember prompts that help to counter the effects of sensory shutdown and enable us to execute things we'd do naturally in less pressured circumstances.

When public speaking, for example, a sequence of 'Cue cards, audience, speak' would describe what no doubt usually happens implicitly, but when you are suffering from sensory shutdown, when it *feels* like you can't recognize a face in the crowd and your vision is tunnelling down to just the prompts on your cards, it can be useful to take a moment to remember your sequence: look up after the cue card, make eye contact with someone at the back of the room and then speak.

Such prompts can be utilized to help us cope with any pressured period. We used as an earlier example the office worker suffering growing sensory shutdown after taking on a huge project, first abandoning their administration and then, once the pressure increased, neglecting meetings and emails (communication) and then eventually personal aspects such as exercise and family time (navigation). By creating personal 'sequences' to anchor our routine ('Attend gym session at lunchtime, clear inbox and write report by 6 p.m., home by 7 for an hour with the kids before their bedtime') we can prevent the narrowing of our focus that lets our own planes fly us.

Once the pressure situation we're dealing with starts affecting our personal lives, exercise is often the first casualty. But exercise is vital if we are to deal with stress and perform better under pressure. Abandoning it is effectively weakening ourselves when we most need to be fit.

Try to treat exercise as you would an important meeting. Even when you have a mountain of work to tackle or you're involved in a big project, time spent keeping fit should be viewed as an appointment you can't postpone. Similarly, plan to leave work at a certain hour and stick to it. Always working to a deadline lets you plan your day more efficiently and you won't find yourself staying late at work.

This approach has the added benefit that you will have time to spend with your family, go out and see friends or even just have some 'you' time in front of the television, listening to music, reading a book or whatever it is you do to relax. Making time for your family and for yourself outside work will, just like exercising, benefit you during a stressful period. It's your navigation; it will allow you to reset, switch off from your work and recharge, so that you can bring your full focus and awareness to the job the next day.

It's very common for people facing a huge workplace challenge to undergo sensory shutdown and rearrange their lives to cope with the pressure situation. But they usually just end up putting more time into it – working ten- or twelve-hour days – rather than more *effective* time. An efficient eight-hour working day will produce more and better results than an unfocused eleven hours of toil, and sticking to our personal deadlines allows us to maintain the framework of our routine – our day-to-day sequencing – so that we're not completely overthrowing our lives because of work pressure. Instead, much like the pilot, we will be better equipped to deal with our own kind of sensory shutdown.

Of course, not everyone has the luxury of being able to set personal deadlines. Junior doctors have little choice but to work long days at hours not of their choosing, as do people who work shifts or are on call. Nevertheless, it is vital to adhere to at least some of our personal sequencing, to find time for family and personal priorities.

Even those with more freedom in their jobs will sometimes have to compromise – maybe only getting out for that cycle ride a couple of times a week instead of the usual five while under pressure. But that's better than nothing – the plane still isn't flying you – and so long as the situation remains both temporary and under your control it's fine in the circumstances. Just as the pilot can't navigate or communicate at 100 per cent efficiency in a trying situation, neither should you expect to.

Beyond Match

In his book *The Gift of Fear*, security specialist Gavin de Becker discusses the importance of training under stress over and over again – to match conditions and even beyond. When training security guards for public figures, he puts them through a process he calls 'stress inoculation'. One exercise involves confronting the security guard with a ferocious dog. Their heart rate is so high when this first happens – above 175 – that, according to de Becker, they can't even see straight. But after repeatedly facing the dogs, and often deliberately commentating, their heart rate starts to become more controllable, so that once it gets down to the 110–20 mark, they're in a much better state to manage their fine motor skills. In this case, they are likely to be applied to using a weapon.

This stress inoculation is, of course, similar to that which trainee pilots undergo. Their training takes them beyond where they are likely to need to go in a real operation, much like we talked in Chapter 1 about going beyond what *feels* right when we practise so that we're better prepared for the real thing.

For the pilot, this means not only an increase in the dislocation of their expectations – new and unpredictable aspects of the operation being thrown in – but also a decrease in the amount of time they're given. If they're coping with a lead time of ten seconds, cut it down to eight. Then when they adjust to that, cut it down again. This will put them in their ugly zone at first, but they will adapt to conditions more changeable and under greater time pressure than those they would reasonably expect to encounter on a real operation.

Take our earlier example of a cricketer learning to face a 90-mph ball using a bowling machine. I've sometimes increased the machine's speed gradually, without disclosing exactly what the speed was. Usually, when it gets up around the 90 mph mark, the batsman struggles initially but then starts making the adjustments implicitly and copes better. By the end of the session the ball is being delivered at over 90 mph – beyond what they'd reasonably expect to face in the match environment – and they're coping really quite well. But the best reaction comes when I tell them just how fast the bowling was that they've been facing – they can scarcely believe it.

The principle is the same as de Becker's: to provide some stress inoculation against facing fast bowling for real, so that in the match environment the player won't experience sensory shutdown.

Buying Time

Ultimately, when it comes to delaying the onset of sensory shutdown, what we're effectively doing is buying ourselves a little time – or at least the *feeling* that we have time. Time to make an effective decision, to respond to an imminent threat or challenge, to look up and address our audience or pick out a player on our team.

In the first chapter we talked about sports performers who appear to have all the time in the world to make the right decision. This, of course, is a skill they've acquired through practice, but part of that skill is their ability to deal with sensory shutdown. If we look at a footballer with the ball at his feet, we could plot a sensory shutdown diagram much as we did for the fighter pilot (Figure 5).

Central to the footballer's priorities under pressure is the ball at his feet: this is his plane to fly. But outside of this comes the necessity to move away from the opposing players – his most

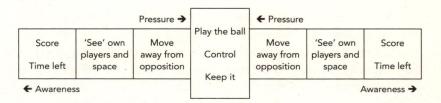

Figure 5

imminent threat in his environment. If he holds on to the ball too long, the other team will surround him and try to dispossess him. His reaction could be to shield the ball or try a bit of skill to get past them – or hit a pass, which would involve the next part in his awareness, seeing his own players and space. Finally, comes the admin, the game situation: what the score is and how long is left to play.

Top players can address all these concerns comfortably, often knowing exactly where their teammates are and what their opponents are likely to do as the ball comes towards them, and they are able to make the correct decision either to keep the ball or play a first-time pass. Their trained awareness makes them look as though they have all day to decide – their skill has effectively allowed them to buy time – but, as we have seen, even they can crack under extreme pressure.

Only the very best, the Messis and Ronaldos, never seem to succumb: no matter how much pressure they're under, they remain apparently immune to sensory shutdown and continue to make good decisions almost instantly.

We can construct a similar diagram for the car salesman I mentioned coaching in Chapter 2, examining how sensory shutdown would affect him (Figure 6). The salesman's starting point is doing his own job, the central act of making sales to people in the car showroom. The next aspect for any salesman is looking for the next sale, doing the groundwork through networking or following up with phone calls. After that is his communicating with colleagues, so they can work in harmony as a united, cohesive team. Finally, comes the admin. Naturally, when the pressure is on this is the first to go, which is why it's a common complaint in sales teams that, when sales people are under extreme pressure to meet their targets, they just focus on their own job and leave others to pick up the pieces – inevitably the admin.

Once sensory shutdown affects him to the point that he isn't communicating with his colleagues any more, the customer perception of the company is likely to be one of 'the left hand

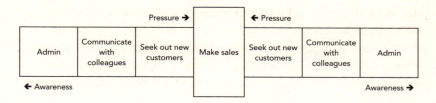

Figure 6

doesn't know what the right is doing'. Chaos, rather than coord-ination, becomes the order of the day. And as the salesman finds himself neglecting the groundwork for future sales – becoming less aware of the essential navigation his role demands – he's back to just flying his plane. If he was better able to manage the groundwork and communicating with colleagues, coordinating the team efforts more, he would find that this would see him wasting less time repeating efforts that colleagues might already have made and buy him more time to prepare future sales, which would make his sales targets all the more achievable in the long run.

Craig looked like he had all the time in the world in the air-craft and that was because his training had given him the skills to buy time. And so, when we make our efforts to avoid the kind of sensory shutdown brought about by a stressful time at work, our efforts are similarly to attempt to buy more time. Making sure we attend that one session at the gym and then get some family time afterwards provides markers to plan our day around, giving us the feeling that we too have bought more time and that we're better managing the aspects of our sequencing.

Flying Your Plane

When we're under pressure, there is a continual tension between the onset of sensory shutdown and effective performance and decision-making. Table 6 brings together the 'how to' aspects of delaying its impact.

Some are more relevant to the likes of a fighter pilot than they are to, say, a golfer, while others might be more useful when driving a car than when playing in a football match, but most are universal.

It is our challenge to implement these techniques to help us delay sensory shutdown, which can debilitate us when we need our wits about us most. The greater our awareness, the more we are able to delay its effects, through taking up command posture to manage the physical impact of anxiety; through self-talk if we need it – either in our heads or out loud – to help us focus; through sequencing the less-critical layers of our performance that we often need to keep aware of even under duress; by doing our best to keep a lower heart rate, whether that's by going beyond match in your preparation, keeping fit through regular exercise or just taking deep, controlled breaths to take on more oxygen and calm us before we take to the match environment.

In this way we can improve our control in the pressured environments we face, rather than having the environment control us. Through managing these facets and practising them we will navigate, communicate and administrate effectively when flying our own plane.

Table 6 Delaying the effects of sensory shutdown

Accelerate	SENSORY SHUTDOWN IMPACT	Delay
Little	◄—— AWARENESS ——►	Greater
Rounded/hunched	◄—— POSTURE ——►	Command
Garbled/non-existent	◄—— SELF-TALK ——►	Deliberate/controlled
Intermittent	◄—— SEQUENCING ——►	Continuous
Higher	◄—— HEART RATE ——►	Lower
Shallow/fast	◄—— BREATHING ——►	Deep/controlled

Principle 7: Sensory Shutdown

The ability to delay the onset of sensory shutdown will dramatically improve your ability both to make decisions and to perform under pressure.

8. THINKING CORRECTLY UNDER PRESSURE

8.

Jumping Off

You're standing on the ledge of a building, fifty storeys high, with the wind howling around you. You look down – down, down, down – at the ant-like people walking the streets below, the toy cars driving down the street – and then you gaze across the five-foot gap to the building opposite: your landing pad. You steady yourself, preparing for your standing long jump to the other building. How on earth did you end up here?

You practised hard at ground level, some 400 feet below, on a small puddle, only a couple of feet across. You got your tech-nique nailed, swinging your arms to create momentum, bending your knees, leaning forward and then propelling yourself into the jump. You reached the point of no return each time, but the stakes were low – just wet feet to worry about.

You then tried a bigger puddle, five feet across, and, while it certainly made things more taxing, you mastered it and began clearing six-foot and even seven-foot puddles. You had wet heels by the end, where you'd just fallen short on occasion, but you'd gone beyond match as you made jumps far in excess of the mere five feet you'd need up in the sky. You discovered that when there is total commitment to the process, the outcome is successful. You were ready to take the ultimate leap of faith.

So now, on top of this skyscraper, you make yourself big and assume command posture in an effort to turn your anxiety into excitement – to mobilize your butterflies. You start to swing your arms, knowing that you must lean forward to the point of no return before you jump: you'll have to commit fully to the process. It's a process you've executed successfully countless times at ground level, when the outcome was far less crucial, but now the only possible outcomes are either life or certain death, your thoughts are turning to the consequences of failure. Your heart is pounding and you close your eyes and breathe deeply, exhaling slowly, while you imagine a successful result. You concentrate on your sequence, your process key: 'See the landing spot, tip over and fire the legs'.

You open your eyes: it's time. You tip forward and launch yourself forward, all the while trying to suppress that inner scream and *not look down*. You hang in mid-air for what seems like an eternity before you touch down on the other side, a good couple of feet clear of the edge. Your legs, with the adrenaline surge subsiding, suddenly feel weak and you collapse to your knees in relief. Congratulations. You committed to the process and the outcome took care of itself.

Process vs Outcome

Focusing on the process rather than the outcome is the essence of performing well under pressure. The tension between process and outcome seems to heighten in proportion to the amount of pressure someone is under to achieve, or, to look at it another way, the significance of not being successful. The more there is at stake, the more likely that thoughts about the outcome will interfere with thoughts about the process. When you were jumping over puddles, with little pressure, it was much easier to commit fully to the process. But once you were fifty storeys high, that all changed, fears about the consequences of failure flooding into your mind. How could they not?

But this doesn't just apply to matters of life and death. This is the conflict that every performer goes through when dealing with pressure: how do I commit to the process in such a way that I don't allow any thoughts about the outcome to pollute my thinking? Throughout this chapter we will expand upon some of the ideas we first touched on in Chapter 4 (Implicit–Explicit Balance) and Chapter 5 (Behaviour), to provide a method for thinking correctly under pressure, or T-CUP.

To be clear, when we talk about concentrating on the process, we're not talking about every aspect of the process. We're not talking about every aspect of your jumping sequence at the top of the building or all the components of your golf swing. We're talking about those conscious process keys that will fill your thoughts. And it is by removing the outcome – putting the net three feet in front of the rugby goal kicker when practising – that we can allow ourselves to give our full attention to the process. This is as true when practising as it is when performing a skill for real: if we trust to our process, the outcome will take care of itself.

This is why we must revisit the power of effective practice. It is through continually practising with consequence – your match practice – that you can build trust in your process, so that you can make this commitment to it when the occasion and the consequences threaten to distract you when under pressure.

The fundamental principle when practising any skill is to create a process based on one or two conscious thoughts that will enable you subconsciously to perform several other actions. The thoughts should be simple to understand, but also fully engaging, so that the concentration involved leaves little or preferably no spare mental capacity to think of anything else, such as the outcome – or the actions that belong in the subconscious.

Back at the 1995 Rugby World Cup, England were playing Australia in the quarter-final, with the Southern Hemisphere team leading 22–19 five minutes from the final whistle, when a penalty was awarded to England. One kick for Rob Andrew, England's fly half, to keep his team, his country, in the match. He waited patiently for the kicking tee to be brought to the field, then lined up his kick. He stepped forward and thumped it with his right foot and the ball went straight between the posts. His conscious thoughts under all that pressure? Simply 'Hard foot and precise piece of stitching'.

This was Rob's way of getting a total focus on the process, rather than indulging any thoughts about the outcome. This has echoes of Harvey Penick's advice to take 'dead aim' at the smallest possible target. For a golfer, this conscious thought might be to hit a specific dimple on the ball. If the player is able to 'see it' (the target) in their mind's eye, then they should be able to become completely engaged with their own unique conscious thoughts. This would be useful to Tom back in Chapter 5 when preparing food for his in-laws, and to you as you stand fifty storeys high preparing to jump. Once we become totally engaged in the process, we can then displace thoughts about the sources of our anxiety – our worry about the outcome – and perform closer to our best. We can all do it. In fact, it can be as easy as driving a car once you know how.

Driving the Car

If we look at the three categories of driver – learner, novice, experienced – we can see big differences in their thought process when under pressure (Figure 7).

For the learner, initially every aspect of the process requires deliberate conscious thought: the accelerator, the brake, the clutch, gears – everything. Mastering these individual components to work in unison, not to mention steering in the right direction, requires a good deal of practice time and no shortage of angst in the ugly zone. This is why most beginners start in an empty car park or on a very quiet road.

As the beginner improves and the core driving skills are practised repeatedly, they hack their way through their forest

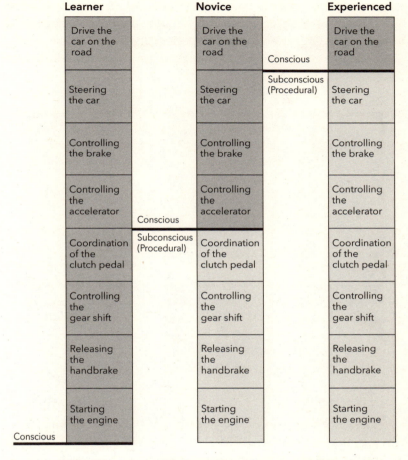

Figure 7 *How thought processes change with experience*

sufficiently often to reach their comfort zone, where they begin
to absorb these aspects into their subconscious – what some like
to call their procedural memory – so that they can be performed
implicitly. The driving test is passed and the learner becomes a
qualified, though still novice, driver. The novice is able to coordinate the clutch and gear stick instinctively, though they still

use their 'Mirror, signal, manoeuvre' self-talk in their heads and their braking and accelerating remain deliberate, conscious actions until they have gained experience.

The experienced driver has absorbed almost all the skills into

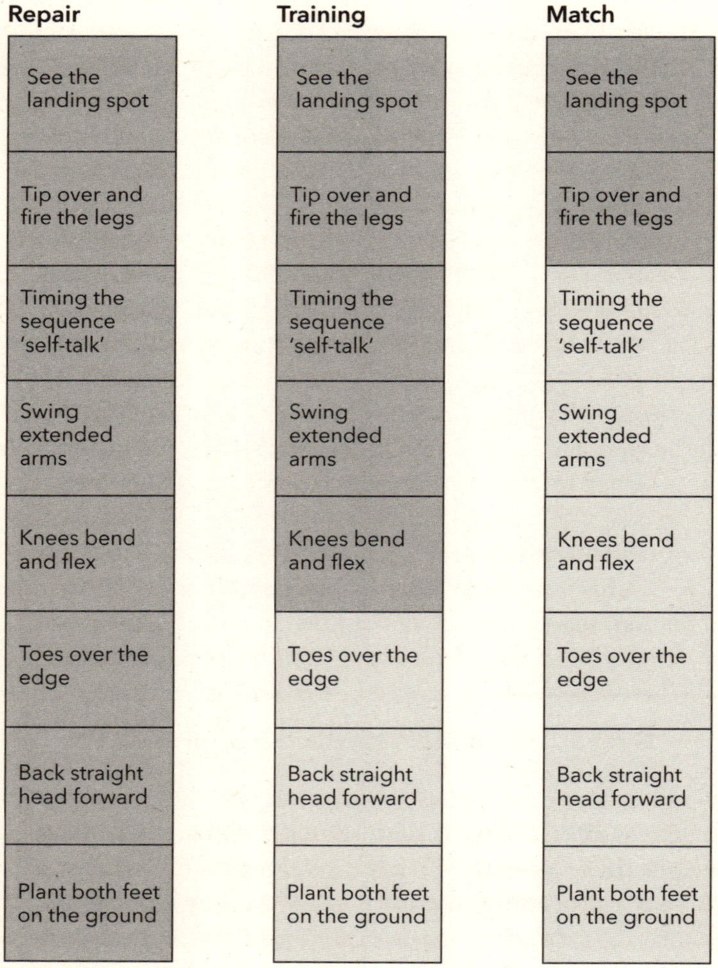

Repair	Training	Match
See the landing spot	See the landing spot	See the landing spot
Tip over and fire the legs	Tip over and fire the legs	Tip over and fire the legs
Timing the sequence 'self-talk'	Timing the sequence 'self-talk'	Timing the sequence 'self-talk'
Swing extended arms	Swing extended arms	Swing extended arms
Knees bend and flex	Knees bend and flex	Knees bend and flex
Toes over the edge	Toes over the edge	Toes over the edge
Back straight head forward	Back straight head forward	Back straight head forward
Plant both feet on the ground	Plant both feet on the ground	Plant both feet on the ground

Figure 8 *Repair, training and match progression*

their procedural memory through hours of committed practice. The only conscious thought they need is simply 'drive the car'. Within this, of course, would be navigation (steering), the communication (taking notice of signals and signs) and administration (the fuel gauge, the speedometer). When an experienced driver needs to improve an aspect of their performance, perhaps they have moved from the country to a city and need to park in tighter spaces than they are used to, they would go through a process of repair in which they would consciously work on those aspects of their driving that usually sit in the subconscious, until they are back in their comfort zone and the ability to park precisely becomes a subconscious procedure.

If we return to the fifty-storey building-to-building jump, we can construct a similar diagram using the familiar labels of repair, training and match (Figure 8). In your repair, when you worked regularly on the individual component – arm swing, forward lean, leg extension and the rest – all of it was conscious thought. Then, when you repeated it and eventually went through the process of clearing larger puddles repeatedly, many of the components were dropped into your subconscious, so that when you reached 'match' you could test the effectiveness of the conscious thoughts that bring it all together under pressure. On top of the building, your conscious thoughts were: *See the landing spot, tip over and fire the legs.*

So, if we look at Figures 7 and 8, the columns on the right represent the effective balance of conscious to subconscious thought when you are thinking correctly under pressure. Not everyone's chart will look exactly the same, of course. They'll be couched in language and specific actions unique to you. But the principle is the same as you progress from novice to expert. Your conscious thoughts are your own formula for success.

T-CUP

It was a hot afternoon in 1999 in Ballymore Stadium in Brisbane, Australia, and things were not going well. Sometimes it just doesn't click when we're trying to execute a skill we can usually do effortlessly: a golfer can 'lose' their swing; you could be taking all day to write up a report that would usually take an hour, tops; and on this occasion Jonny Wilkinson was struggling with his sequence and feel. We were experiencing a bit of a block in the blazing Australian sun, a paralysis of analysis, when I decided to change tack.

I walked to the stand behind the goalposts and put a rugby top across the back of a seat. I explained to Jonny that this was Doris. She didn't particularly like rugby but her husband regularly dragged her to games. Doris was ignoring the game; she was instead absorbed in a magazine and I challenged Jonny to kick the ball to knock the magazine out of her hands, but not hit her. Jonny set the ball down and focused his whole attention on this smallest of targets.

The first kick landed within a couple of feet of Doris, but once he got into a rhythm, Doris was being bombarded. 'I just hit the magazine out of her hands,' he announced.

'OK, this time go for the can of cola on her armrest,' I replied. The barrage continued. 'Now she's eating an ice cream. Knock the ice cream off but don't hit the cone!'

On it went. The session lasted for nigh on two hours as Jonny rediscovered his kicking mojo, thanks to Doris. This emphasis on the smallest possible target had put all thoughts about technique back in the subconscious, where they belonged. In essence, it became the perfect practice T-CUP formula. If he aimed for Doris with his kick, the outcome would take care of itself.

Your T-CUP is your shorthand note to yourself, your conscious thought to engage you in your process. If we go back to when you were struggling on the squash court, your T-CUP formula could have been, 'Bounce, hit'. If we return to Tom and his dinner party with the in-laws, he would have had a series of T-CUP formulas, such as: 'Check the food in the oven, keep topping up glasses', 'Talk to the guests' and then 'Keep an eye on the pan while preparing the salad', each of them different actions and thought processes that had a level of detail he was able to execute subconsciously. In the repair stage of his progress, he would have been flooded with many more conscious thoughts about things he no longer needs to think about now.

That's the point about the T-CUP formula: it doesn't constantly stay the same. Rob Andrew's 'Hard foot and precise bit of stitching' wasn't the first we'd produced together. It was the result of the hours of practice – the repair, training and match – he'd put in that meant his formula was able to be reduced to this short, sharp phrase, which fired a lot of other subconscious movements.

The reason it's a formula is because we test it in our match preparation to see whether it's effective. If it's not, we hone it until it is. Just like the affirmations back in Chapter 2, they're always being adapted or even changed completely to allow subconscious procedures to be performed at their best under pressure. The power of effective language, individually tailored, again cannot be overstated in developing these formulas.

As you improve at anything, your T-CUP formula will naturally change. Just like you, it's continually adapting. A specific thought that may have been conscious a month or two ago will now be wrapped up in another word or phrase that addresses a different part of your process. A good example of this is posture. We talked at length at the beginning of this book about the need to reset your posture for pressure events, be it for a drinks reception at work, before you meet the in-laws or on the starting line of the race you've entered. But as you get used to doing this and deliberately resetting your posture each time, you'll find that, in a process of repair, training and match, you're doing it subconsciously and you'll no longer need to include it in your formula. Your T-CUP will evolve just as you evolve.

The more engaging your T-CUP is for your conscious mind, the more you'll be able to avoid the destructive thoughts about outcome that inevitably arise when the pressure's on. Ultimately, it is this worry about the outcome – this fear of failure – that is the source of most performance anxiety.

Winning the Lottery

In 1998 the England football team, under the management of Glenn Hoddle, arrived in France with high hopes. They made it through to the quarter-finals against old foes Argentina, where, despite David Beckham's by now infamous sending off, they held on to draw the match 2–2 and faced the so-called 'lottery' of the penalty shootout. England had form here, having exited both the World Cup in 1990 and the European Championships in 1996 at the semi-final stage on penalties. It was to be an all too familiar script, as England midfielders Paul Ince and David Batty, who took the decisive penalty to keep England in the shootout, both missed. England were out.

No book about pressure would be complete without addressing the penalty shootout in football. It has been labelled a 'lottery' and an unfitting way to settle a high-stakes football match – a challenge of pot luck after a two-hour contest. Well, there is a saying that does the rounds in golf: 'The more I practise, the luckier I get.'

The reason for picking on England's exit in 1998 is partly because of the fact that David Batty had never taken a penalty in a senior game, which perhaps made him something of an odd choice, though, to be fair, there weren't many options remaining on the pitch – but it's largely because the squad apparently didn't practise penalties. Glenn Hoddle has said since that he thinks the idea that 'we just need to practise penalties more in order to prevent another exit' is ridiculous. He cites the long walk up to take the penalty, the particularly unique set of pressured circumstances that can't be replicated in training and during which doubt enters the players' heads, as being the biggest factor in England's failures (they lost shootouts in 1990, 1996, 1998, 2004, 2006 and 2012).

If there's one thing this book should have made clear by now, it is the power of effective practice to enable us to perform better under pressure. While it is true that the absolute match environment cannot be created in training, surely it's still worth putting in the time to practise rather than not hitting any at all? And besides, with imagination you can do your best to get closer to the real thing. When I work with rugby teams or golfers, we don't have thousands of spectators or the exact match-day conditions in which to practise, but there is still huge benefit to be had in repair and training – hitting penalties over and over again to put aspects of them in the subconscious mind – and with a bit of creativity, steps can be taken to make the practice more realistic. If the walk from the halfway line is such a factor, couldn't penalties be practised in this manner, with all the players in the centre circle and the penalty taker making his lonely march to the spot?

In some respects you can make the practice even more demanding than the match conditions. In rugby I spend a lot of time with international players in which they kick from very narrow angles, which reduces the target to about a tenth of the size it would be in a match. Another method is to give the players a series of kicks from different positions on the field. If one is missed in the sequence, they have to start again. In football, having penalty targets in specific parts of the net will hone in the skill and expose any technical flaws in a player's technique. This will enable you to create some very relevant repair work (technique) for penalty taking where the criteria are accuracy and pace of the kick to beat the goalkeeper.

As we illustrated in the C to J concept, the physical impact of pressure has a tendency to move the player towards a tighter,

C-shape trajectory, with the pillar rotating. When this happens with penalty taking, the player is in danger of wrapping the ball on the inside of his leg swing, which often gives the goalkeeper an easier opportunity to save. Or, even more destructively, a very tight C-shape will lead to the ball escaping to the right (if the kicker is right-footed). The J-shape kicker gets his power and commitment from his body shift towards the target, and under pressure he is using the biggest muscle group possible to make the kick. Couple that with command posture (helping to produce a productive mindset) and they are far more likely to direct the ball accurately. The caveat is that it will only happen as a result of consistent, measured practice.

Then there is also the importance of excitement and vibe within practice sessions to create a can-do attitude and get players to commit regularly to their ugly zone. If we were to look at shooting at a specific spot in the corner of a net, how many players would be encouraged to practise regularly, little and often, and genuinely celebrate progress and achievement?

If David Batty had never taken a penalty in a senior game, then he had no match experience to call upon. Practice would have been his only crutch – the only thing that could even begin to prepare him for the experience he was about to face. It's difficult to understand how, of the ten England internationals still on the pitch, there weren't enough to take five penalties effectively. Football is a chaotic, unpredictable environment and to be caught unprepared would suggest that the football team made the same mistake as the England rugby team in the 1995 World Cup, when Jonah Lomu burst on to the scene, in not effectively preparing for the possibility of dislocated expectations.

No less an expert than former England striker and regular penalty taker Gary Lineker has talked about the necessity of practising penalties: 'It's like saying a golfer never practises a six-foot putt. Yes, it's different when it's for the Open Championship, but it doesn't half help if you've actually hit a few.'

T-CUP is represented in Figure 9. This figure does assume a

Productive ↑		Conscious / Subconscious (Procedural)			Conscious / Subconscious (Procedural memory)	Negative ↓
Can-do thoughts	Conscious	See the precise target	See the precise target			Destructive thoughts
- Butterflies in formation	Subconscious (Procedural)	Zone in on the piece of stitching	Zone in on the piece of stitching			- I hope I don't miss
- I feel great		Crush the ball	Crush the ball			- What will my friends say?
- I'm going to break the net						- I feel sick
- I really mean this! (aggression)		Posture: Tall neck	Posture: Tall neck			- I don't want to be the one to fail
- I know I can, I have practised so hard		Body over impact	Body over impact			- I must remember to crush the ball with my laces, approach at 45° and keep my neck straight
- I am in command (posture)		Laces on the ball	Laces on the ball			
- The target is so big		Kicking foot down	Kicking foot down			- I must not miss
- This is going to be great		45° approach	45° approach	Conscious		- I can't jump this gap
- I can jump the gap – I will clear it by 2 feet		Follow along	Follow along	Subconscious (Procedural memory)		- I don't want to fall

Figure 9 *T-CUP under pressure*

degree of expertise. The two centre columns show a penalty-taker's thought processes. In the left-hand column, there are only the two conscious thoughts, the T-CUP formula: *See the precise target* and *Zone in on the piece of stitching*, for the player who is filled with productive, can-do thoughts before he sets himself to shoot; however, the right-hand column describes a player filled with destructive, negative thoughts. In short, the player is in no fit state of mind to perform well under pressure.

Kickers should be aspiring to be in the left-hand column and this can only be achieved by the kind of practice that gives confidence in the process, so that the outcome can be trusted to take care of itself. The kind of confidence that Jonny Wilkinson, Rob Andrew and Johnny Sexton were able to call upon. Furthermore, when watching the England football team's missed penalties in shootouts, it's clear that, unlike Rob, Johnny and Jonny, they have a haphazard pre-shot routine. It appears to be, 'Get the ball down and get it over with as soon as possible', rather than deliberately placing the ball, seeing the precise target and smashing the ball past the goalkeeper. Compare that with a rugby player, where they take a deep breath, slow things down and set themselves properly for the shot before executing aggressively.

By using a similar process, a footballer would have a better chance of managing the impact of their anxiety and delaying any sensory shutdown. It would also displace those interfering conscious thoughts, moving them back down into the subconscious where they belong. Do all this and, the next time they find themselves in a penalty shootout, who knows?

Displacement Training

The long walk from the centre circle to take a penalty in a shootout offers players an opportunity to do something they could manage well without: overthinking. On that walk they have time to think about where to put their kick, but also plenty of time to think about the outcome, about the consequences of failure. Golf is no different, especially when the pressure is on. Players have a long gap between shots while they walk to their ball, plenty of time for similarly negative thoughts. Perhaps it was this overthinking that inspired Mark Twain to say, 'Golf is a good walk spoiled.' Perhaps Twain was simply struggling to manage his anxiety between shots!

If we look at pressure situations in our own lives, we often have plenty of time to overthink them beforehand too. When we're lying in bed at night, with work or meeting the in-laws or running the 5k the next day, it's easy to fill our heads with worry as we walk towards the 'penalty spot'. Overthinking can be as detrimental to our own performance as it can to a sports performer, who would start second-guessing and unpicking their technique, forcing things that belong in their subconscious above the line into conscious thought. We can deprive ourselves of sleep worrying about it beforehand and when the occasion arrives, things that we would usually do implicitly – make small talk with the in-laws, make eye contact in an interview or presentation at the right moments – we're suddenly extremely conscious of. We could become awkward, stumbling over our words, looking down at the floor.

I don't believe it's possible to train people *not* to think about something. Remember that purple elephant I asked you not to think about? Instead, we need to find something to displace the potentially destructive thoughts. For Jonny Wilkinson practising on the rugby field, it was Doris. Focusing on her magazine, her ice-cream cone, all helped displace the thoughts about technique he was struggling with so he was able to function at the effective level of conscious thought.

We are able to do this in our own lives. When you hear of people throwing themselves into their work during periods of personal stress, this is the same: they are displacing stressful thoughts with immediate thoughts of work. And we can do this to a less dramatic degree with some of the pressure situations we all have to face. Time pressures often make this difficult, but if we're able to prepare for our interview or presentation in advance, so that we're not working on it right up until we go to bed the night before, we can instead do something like watch a film, read a book or see friends or family, and this can act as a gentle displacement exercise, to focus our thoughts elsewhere in the build-up to the event.

In Ben Lyttleton's book *Twelve Yards*, German footballer Stefan Kuntz describes a more aggressive method of thought displacement when he was preparing to take his penalty, the fifth, in the Euro '96 semi-final against England:

> *'During that walk, you are so alone, so afraid. I had to find a way to conquer my nerves. So I made myself angry. That way, I forgot about the nerves.' Kuntz thought about his children, who were then five and seven, and how their school-mates would tease them if he missed the penalty. 'I got so angry at the thought of these clowns upsetting my kids. I thought, "Don't do this to your family!"'*

Needless to say, Kuntz aggressively buried his penalty and England were soon out of the tournament when Gareth Southgate, who had not practised penalties, missed his. Kuntz's method of displacing his thoughts might sound unusual, but it was effective He wasn't thinking about his kicking technique; he was instead focusing on his anger. You might say that, instead of turning his anxiety into excitement, he turned it into anger, which produced a real focused aggression. And that's the point with the T-CUP formula and in our efforts to displace our own unhelpful thoughts: it needs to be personal to us. For Kuntz, it was his family.

You will need to find your own bespoke method of displacing unhelpful thoughts so that you can think correctly under pressure. It will take some trial and error, just like it did for Jonny and Rob, but this is what your match practice is for. When you find the right formula you might not even realize it at first, because quite often we're not aware of what we're *not* thinking about.

But you'll see the improvement in your performance and you'll begin to trust yourself.

New Balls, Please!

Elite sportsmen and women spend years working on their skills to be able to perform them on the biggest stage. Once their processes are honed and they are thinking correctly under pressure, then it should be the case that, if they do their processes right and perform to the best of their ability, they will get their intended outcome. Of course, even then they might be beaten on the day by better opposition, but there is no shame in that. What is difficult to accept, however, is when the equipment lets you down.

A top performer needs to be able to trust implicitly in their equipment. Golfers spend hours sourcing clubs and balls that give them consistent results; tennis players do likewise with the setup of their rackets; even footballers need the ball to be of the requisite standard for them to execute their skills effectively in front of the thousands of fans who have paid good money to see them do so. And it's for this reason that I was so disappointed by the Rugby World Cup in New Zealand in 2011.

Like every other team, we were provided with tournament balls to use in training. I noticed initially that some of the balls didn't seem right: the strike – the feel reported by the players – and the flight weren't true, although this seemed to improve with use.

England won our first pool game narrowly, 13–9, against a very spirited Argentinian XV, but the goal kicking from both sides was well below standard. Jonny Wilkinson missed five kicks, while Argentina, who used two kickers, missed six in total. The game was played in an indoor stadium, so there was no wind factor, and although one kicker having a bad game might be understandable, for all three to do so in an environment unaffected by the weather was highly unusual.

Why did this happen? The simple fact is that the match balls were inconsistent. Eight match balls are supplied for every game (when the ball goes into the stands another is used to keep the play flowing), and when we used them the day before during the team run in the stadium, not all of them behaved the same in the air. For the kicker, this plays havoc with the mental side of their game. Instead of thinking, 'If I do this [process], I will get that [outcome],' they start to think, 'If I do this, I *might* get that.' The implicit trust in their equipment has been lost and their ability to think correctly under pressure compromised.

The day after the game I took a bag of brand-new balls and spent several hours kicking on my own. It was clear that some of them were behaving differently, despite being straight out of the packet. They needed a good few days' kicking in before they were fit for a match, which wasn't going to happen. I reported my findings to the head coach, Martin Johnson, and Rob Andrew, by then the RFU's director of rugby, and made suggestions as to what we could do to manage the situation – to work with our dislocated expectations.

Mindful that we would always be playing with brand-new balls in the matches, we did likewise in training for our next game, against Georgia. During the team run in the stadium, when we were working with the new match balls, we'd test them using the Top Pocket system. As the match balls were numbered 1 to 8, we were able to note the characteristics of each ball – and so identify those we were keenest to avoid. We'd confirm our findings in the warm-up on match day and where possible during the game we tried to keep the best balls on the pitch.

Against Georgia we fared better, winning relatively comfortably with Toby Flood missing only two kicks from a possible seven. In our next game, against Romania, we did the same. On this occasion the players identified ball number 5 as a 'real dog'. Frustratingly, this ball seemed to be in play throughout most of the match, and Toby Flood missed a kick with it in the second half. After that, we took the ball out of action, hiding it behind the hoardings, so it couldn't be used by either side. Unbeknown to me, a match official had reported both myself and Bobby Stridgeon, the England fitness coach, who had actually kicked number 5 away and given Jonny a different ball in the first half, for breaking a law of the game. Bobby was simply doing what I asked him to and, in my opinion, should not have been implicated.

In the build-up to England's game against Scotland, we walked right into a disciplinary storm. The Rugby World Cup organization were investigating the incident to see if Bobby and I were guilty of misconduct, as it is not permitted to switch balls when a player kicks a conversion without permission from the referee, and the English RFU had lengthy discussions with them about the matter, which I knew little about. I was left with a choice: either accept a one-match ban or attend a hearing on the Saturday (match day), which would mean both Wilkinson and Flood having to attend it too. Hardly ideal preparation for the match. I felt that this was no choice at all, so I accepted the ban.

The press, naturally, had a field day – Ballgate! I still maintain that I did nothing wrong: tennis players change balls all the time and there are other instances in a rugby match when it is permitted to change the ball, such as when the hooker wants a dry ball to throw into the lineout. Out-of-shape cricket balls are routinely replaced. I have since been told that both Scotland and South Africa also complained about the balls.

Why did this matter so much to me? Well, at this level, consistency in the equipment isn't just important, it's crucial. There is enough for a performer to think about when the pressure's on without having additional interfering thoughts about the equipment to deal with. It is much tougher to commit fully to a process that only *might* produce the intended outcome. If we go back to that five-foot jump between fifty-storey buildings, how would it affect you if the concrete edging was crumbling and unstable? A little piece breaks off and falls all the way down to the ground: how ready are you to commit to the process now?

Equipment inconsistency causes the player to start unpicking their subconscious thoughts. When results become inconsistent they'll start to blame themselves when, in fact, it is the equipment that isn't consistent. Surely both players and fans deserve better?* If you were asked to take your driving test in a car with no brakes, would that be an accurate platform from which to assess your driving capability?

While we can plan for dislocations in our expectations, we should be able to depend on the basics when we perform under pressure, certainly in terms of our equipment. If you work in an office, you would reasonably expect your computer not to crash half a dozen times a day. If you are a doctor or nurse, you would expect your equipment to provide accurate readings. If you are a soldier going into combat, you would certainly expect your weapon to fire when the trigger is pulled.

We need to know that, when we approach a task under pressure, if we do this (the process), then we get that (the outcome). And if we don't, then we need to know for certain it's because of us and not our equipment, so that we can take steps to correct it. I hope this book can do a lot to help you, but it won't be able to fix your brakes or your computer – or repair the cement on the ledge before you make that leap.

Just Hit It

Thinking correctly under pressure is a method for displacing unhelpful thoughts and filling your mind with productive, engaging keys – language here is vital – to help you perform at

---

* There was a solution. The fact was that some of the brand-new match balls still had inconsistent flight patterns after only a few kicks over two days (the match is played on the second day), but after a week all the balls that were supplied began to perform consistently. The answer would have been to give the match balls to the teams for the whole week of the game. On Friday the balls could have been given back to the officials ready for the match. Sadly, I was denied any opportunity to suggest such a solution.

your best. It is a way for you to commit fully to a process you've practised so that you can leave thoughts of the outcome – the major source of all of our performance anxieties – to one side. The outcome will then take care of itself. When we can truly lose ourselves in the process we can appreciate what people mean when they say they're 'in the zone'. We become immersed in our process, acting implicitly and not hugely conscious of much else, and this is what we're all striving for when we perform under pressure.

Your T-CUP is an ever-changing formula that should help you strive to reach this. As you gain experience, so your formula for each task you're attempting will develop; it grows with you. Anyone can use T-CUP, at any stage of their development, just so long as you are prepared to practise. When we look back to John, the little boy having a go at golf back in Chapter 3, we see that he didn't harbour any thoughts about failure. We have *learned* about fearing failure as we've grown older. John didn't need a formula to help organize his mind in the back garden with the ball and club: he just hit it and was excited at the result.

In essence, we're all trying to 'just hit it' – to be completely lost in that wonderful moment, with no unhelpful thoughts about the consequences, no possibility of 'failure' clouding our minds. We need to be able to stand on the ledge and, with excitement, commit wholeheartedly to jumping off.

Principle 8: Thinking Correctly Under Pressure

Focusing on the outcome and its implications rather than the process directly interferes with our ability to perform effectively under pressure.

CONCLUSION

The Pressure Principle

| Anxiety | Managing Learning | Implicit – Explicit Balance | Behaviour | Environment | Sensory Shutdown | Thinking Correctly Under Pressure | Language |

Figure 10 *The Pressure Principle*

The Pressure Principle starts with **Anxiety** because that is the source of the majority of our problems with pressure. It is through our *perception* of a threat, usually in objectively non-threatening circumstances, that our worries about our performance and our stress levels begin to increase. Our nerves produce the physical effects of our anxiety – the butterflies in our stomachs, the tightness in our chests – that can be mobilized and used to our advantage. By understanding and becoming more conscious of the effect our anxieties have upon us, we can, through our body language and posture, turn them into excitement.

It is our use of **Language** that enables us to reframe how we feel about pressure; it is language that allows us to effect this change from anxiety to excitement, so that we can begin to perceive these feelings as high-octane fuel for a great performance. It is language that can boost our self-esteem and raise our confidence – the life-blood for any performer, be it a Premier League footballer or the sixteen-year-old school-leaver starting in the post room. It is language too, in its careless and thoughtless application, that can sadly inhibit and destroy these qualities. So it is through the use of powerful, productive language, of recognizing what we do well and setting our approach in *how* to do well through our affirmations, that we can give ourselves the platform to benefit from all the other aspects.

Managing Learning is simply developing the impetus to commit to improving at our own margin and from our individual starting point. We have to give ourselves the opportunity to commit to the ugly zone, the place where true improvement is made, and repeatedly hack our way through the forest to clear our paths. The ugly zone can be a tough place to be, but it's a place we'll never revisit if we don't inject some enjoyment into proceedings, celebrating our successes and remembering to keep it 'little and often' so we don't burn ourselves out. For those teaching others, the mantra 'The response we get is the meaning of the message' applies. We should always be working from the learner's map of reality, so that we can communicate effectively and empathize accordingly. We've all heard someone say, 'I've told them that a hundred times!' Yes, but have you thought about changing the message?

The weighing scales of our minds is the **Implicit–Explicit Balance**, the importance of learning with the minimum amount of information and performing with the minimum of essential explicit thought. Too many of us attempt to start our improvement by overloading on detail and theory first and build up to the actual execution of a task, rather than having a go first and working on the detail and theory while we do so. Think about assembling flat-pack furniture, about using the information in bite-size, manageable chunks. It's the same when we perform under pressure: thinking too much about aspects of a process we should be doing implicitly will only lead to trouble – and potentially cause a system jam.

The most productive approach to improving any skill is to see it as a **Behaviour** change. Take a leaf out of the dolphins' book and learn to accept and reinforce the behaviour you want to repeat and ignore that which you don't. Once you learn a new behaviour, remember that initially the previous one is just below the surface. In the beginning, it's easy to slip back into old habits, to re-enter the comfort zone, but if we are able to commit to the process of repair, training and match, so that the behaviours we produce when we practise are closer to those we need when we're doing it for real, then we will be as well prepared as possible. Never underestimate the power of effective, deliberate and enjoyable practice.

The importance of the **Environment** in which we perform cannot be overstated. It does as much good for a child to do a full dress rehearsal of a school play on the stage in the main hall as it does for an international rugby team to have their final team run in the stadium in which they are going to play. Familiarizing ourselves with our environment helps narrow the potential for a dislocation in our expectations, so that there are fewer nasty surprises for us when the pressure is really on. But it's not just the match environment that is important: it is the more general environment – the culture – in which we exist. If the company culture where we work is one of inspiring initiative without fear of unnecessary repercussions, then it becomes a much more stable base for us to take measured risks and feel less pressure about the consequences. If the environment at home is one of understanding, support and encouragement, then no matter how pressured things get we have a safe haven to help alleviate the stress and give us the tools to really flourish.

Sensory Shutdown is the inevitable decrease in our awareness as the pressure mounts. Sensory shutdown affects us all, but that doesn't mean we have to be a slave to it. We can delay its impact by adopting a routine that will keep us in the present and allow us to attend to those aspects that might otherwise become lost as the pressure rises and our awareness narrows. Through finding our own way to 'Fly, navigate, communicate, administrate' we can delay the impact of sensory shutdown, which will allow us to manage stress more effectively.

Finally, **Thinking Correctly Under Pressure**, is our formula for *what* to think and *how* to think about it when the pressure is on. Your T-CUP formula is separate from your preparation – your 'pre-shot routine' – and it is the method by which you can fully engage your conscious mind with specific, precise process thoughts and displace those unhelpful, destructive thoughts about the outcome. Your T-CUP develops as you do, and the more you work effectively by using other aspects of the Pressure Principle, the shorter your formula will eventually become. But thinking correctly under pressure isn't just a formula: it's a holistic way to look at our approach to pressure. If we don't tackle it with the right thought processes, then we cannot hope to perform as we'd like.

You *Can* Do This

So there we have it, your recipe for performing under pressure. Of course, a liberal seasoning of the no limits mindset is required, and this is the mindset that underpins every aspect of the Pressure Principle. It is the belief that, whatever your level, no matter where you are now, you can always improve. It is about starting with what you *can* do, not what you can't.

As children, we had no fear about failure, no anxieties about performing under pressure. We didn't really understand what pressure was – we'd have a go at something and if it didn't work, we'd simply try again. We'd throw ourselves into learning without thought of the outcome. We were close to perfect in this way: constantly in the moment, always growing and developing. But as we became adults, we learned about pressure. We learned about failure and its consequences. Many of us grew to *fear* it, to do what we can to avoid it.

It doesn't have to be that way. We might not be able to go back to being children again, but the Pressure Principle can help us do our best to recreate that feeling – to help us conquer our fear of failure and the obsession with outcomes.

The Pressure Principle is a philosophy. It is through organizing our thoughts, and opening up the reciprocal relationship between body and mind, that we can conquer the negative impact of pressure on ourselves. Our performance in pressure moments might well define our lives, but we can use the Pressure Principle to improve our response to these moments.

My biggest hope is that, through reading this book, you can see that dealing with pressure isn't a gift that some are born with, while others must struggle on. Performing under pressure is a skill, just like any other. It is a skill that you can work on and practise to improve. You don't have to come home at the end of the day thinking, *I wish I hadn't let my nerves get the better of me.*

This can be a thing of the past for you. By implementing the Pressure Principle, as you enjoy and celebrate your own success, you'll discover that there really are no limits at the margins of everything you do. You can rekindle that youthful vigour, that fearless, curious approach to challenges – and you *will* rekindle it, if you're prepared to commit. We can all continually improve and enjoy the thrill of getting better.

You can do it. You'll see.

Under Pressure Now

A hush descends. All eyes turn to you. One shot for glory.

You set your feet firmly on the ground and make yourself big. You stretch your neck and set your shoulders into the now familiar command posture. Your butterflies are stirring but you can already feel them starting to fly in formation. Your heart rate is up in expectation; under the watchful eyes of all of your colleagues, you take a deep breath, exhaling slowly.

You take the screwed-up paper ball in your hands – it feels

reassuringly familiar between your palms – and roll it tight. All part of your pre-shot routine. You hold it now in your throwing hand and its weight and size feel so right – you've done this a hundred times before, gone through the process of repair, training and match. Not that you're consciously aware of that right now. You've closed your eyes and you're visualizing the ball of paper landing perfectly in the waste-paper bin. *This is inevitable.* Now you open them, and even that thought is pushed from your mind now as you fill it with your T-CUP formula: *High elbow, forefinger and thumb along the flight.* If you adhere to the process, the outcome will take care of itself.

You take dead aim at the smallest spot in the middle of the bin. You raise your elbow, arm cocked, and then bring it forward to release the ball of paper. It leaves your hand and the room takes a collective intake of breath as it arcs through the air . . .

. . . and lands plumb in the bin, a satisfying *bong!* ringing out like a muffled dinner gong, breaking the silence. A split second of hush ensues and then uproar as you jump to your feet, fists pumping, grinning from ear to ear. Your colleagues have erupted into cheers, whistling and applauding. *You've done it!* Your putt for victory in the Ryder Cup, the last-minute penalty to win a World Cup final – you have made office history.

You feel like a child on Christmas Day, absorbing the adulation with a sense of pride, celebrating what you have achieved, reinforcing what you've done right. It's like being five years old all over again. You are beaming with excitement – not to mention over a thousand pounds better off.

BIBLIOGRAPHY

R. F. Baumeister, E. Bratslavsky, C. Finkenauer and K. D. Vohs, 'Bad Is Stronger Than Good', *Review of General Psychology* 5 (2001): 323–70

Ken Blanchard and Spencer Johnson, *The One Minute Manager: Increase Productivity, Profits and Your Own Prosperity* (HarperCollins, 2011)

Ellis Cashmore, *Sport and Exercise Psychology: The Key Concepts*, 2nd edn (Routledge, 2008)

Gavin de Becker, *The Gift of Fear: Survival Signals that Protect Us from Violence* (Little, Brown, 1997)

Steve Drzewiecki (Traverse City Police Department), 'Survival Stress in Law Enforcement', an applied research project submitted to the Department of Interdisciplinary Technology as part of the School of Police Staff and Command Program, September 20, 2002

John Dunlosky, Katherine A. Rawson, Elizabeth J. Marsh, Mitchell J. Nathan and Daniel T. Willingham, 'Improving Students' Learning with Effective Learning Techniques: Promising Directions from Cognitive and Educational Psychology', *Psychological Science in the Public Interest* 14(1) (2013): 4–58

K. Anders Ericsson, Ralf Th. Krampe and Clemens Tesch-Romer, 'The Role of Deliberate Practice in the Acquisition of Expert Performance', *Psychological Review* 100(3) (1993): 363–406

Timothy Gallwey, *The Inner Game of Tennis: The Ultimate Guide to the Mental Side of Peak Performance*, new edn (Pan, 2015)

Malcolm Gladwell, *Blink: The Power of Thinking Without Thinking* (Little, Brown, 2005)